Life in a Marital Institution

Life in a Marital Institution

Twenty Years of Monogamy in One Terrifying Memoir

James Braly

ST. MARTIN'S PRESS
NEW YORK

Author's Note: There are three types of stories: 1) Reality—where you can imagine it happening to you; 2) Fantasy—where you wish it were happening to you; and 3) Horror—where you're glad it's not happening to you. This is not Reality. And it's not Fantasy. But it happens to be True. I have changed some names and identifying characteristics of certain places and persons to protect their privacy. I also have reconstructed some of the dialogue from memory when I didn't have journal entries, and I have conflated some of the incidents because you simply wouldn't believe me if I told you the whole story.

"The Night I Beat My Inner Loser" first appeared in a different form in *New York Press* in 2002.

"Stand-Up Husband" first appeared in a different form in *New York Press* in 2003.

www.stmartins.com

ISBN 978-0-312-60728-9 (hardcover)
ISBN 978-1-250-02884-6 (e-book)

St. Martin's Press books may be purchased for educational, business, or promotional use. For information on bulk purchases, please contact Macmillan Corporate and Premium Sales Department at 1-800-221-7945 extension 5442 or write specialmarkets@macmillan.com.

First Edition: April 2013

10 9 8 7 6 5 4 3 2 1

For Kathy

CONTENTS

The heart has its reasons that reason knows nothing of.

—Blaise Pascal

Prologue

I once asked my wife, Jane, in a heated moment, after I'd refused to see a fourteenth marriage counselor, "What if we were immortal! You think we'd stay married *forever*?"

She said, "Yes!" Her capacity for conflict—and couples counseling—knew no limits. Taken together with her spiritual beliefs, her commitment to the marriage meant it was not only possible but likely we'd never stop fighting—*ever.*

I loved and admired Jane deeply for that, her loyalty to *us* across infinite time. Even though, if she was right, it portended infinite misery.

And my capacity to experience misery was finite, which—like any emotionally arrested adult—I didn't believe for a long time. Like a child, I thought I was immortal. That I had forever to be unhappy, until one day, magically, I would wake up a happy man in a happy marriage.

Then it finally hit: If I wanted to be happy in *this* lifetime, I would have to live my life differently.

This came as an enormous, irritating shock. I have worn more or less the same clothes, eaten more or less the same food, and listened to exactly the same music since I was a teenager. If I wanted to change myself, I would have started a long time ago. I may not like my life, but I love that it's predictable: This time tomorrow, I *know* I'll be miserable! There is real comfort in that.

Sadly, I could not *not* see that I would have to change. The birth of a new way of seeing, like birth itself, is a lot like death: It cannot be ignored, it changes everything, and it can come when you least expect it.

ONE

Locovore

If God had told me,
"Go down there and find the woman least suited
to walk this earth with you,"
that woman would have been your mother.
—my father

I'm standing on the sidewalk in Blue Hill, a tiny town in upstate New York, hands cupped around my eyes, peering through the plate-glass window of a Victorian house that's been converted into a café, like a thief, or a real estate agent, or—given the crazed reflection looking back at me from the plate glass—an ex-husband spying on his ex-wife. All of which I may become. But first, I need to eat. I'm insane with hunger, having driven around for three hours now, since shortly after breakfast, trying to find food my wife, Jane, will allow our two young boys to eat. So that I can eat.

Jane is very strict about what goes into our boys' bodies, and they are equally strict about what goes into mine: If I get it, they want it, too. Like father, like sons. Fair enough. Except, their mother is my wife. And my wife controls food the way other men's wives control sex: I don't get enough.

To satisfy my hunger, I engage in illicit, secret, gustatory assignations with sundry food mistresses: delis on the corner, drive-through windows, and, this morning, gas stations, leaving my boys strapped in their child seats while I wolf bags of potato chips and Combos in the gas station bathrooms, then (after wiping the crumbs from my face) walk back to the car and feign sympathetic hunger. It worked for a few hours, until I started to feel nauseated by the cottonseed oil, and guilty I was eating while my own flesh and blood starved.

Now I am literally sick to my stomach, in addition to starving. (That's why they're called "empty calories.")

So I'm looking through my finger-tent frame as I lean against the plate-glass window, and I see these words: *local, organic, seasonal.* The Holy Alternative Trinity! My answered prayer! Even the desserts are enlightened: "Sweetened with agave," whatever *that* is. It's the kind of food Jane feeds the family: whole foods for a whole lot of money; everything we've been looking for in lunch, since shortly after breakfast—when Jane and the boys picked me up at the Amtrak station and we embarked on our relaxing drive in the country.

Jane and I moved up from the city recently, and we don't know the culinary landscape yet. So we've been getting to know it together, for the past three hours, driving to and away from every restaurant in a thirty-mile radius. All of which, it turns out, serve "mainstream" food that lots of mainstream people eat—seemingly quite happily, based on what my boys and I saw through various restaurant windows while we looked on from numerous restaurant parking lots and curbsides in hunger and envy.

Until now, when, peering into the "local, organic, seasonal" café, my persistence and patience pay off.

But then I see, written on top of the menu in the plate-glass window, right under "Hours of Operation," that the only "local, organic, seasonal" café in a thirty-mile radius is *"Closed."* Evidently local, organic, seasonal waiters take the afternoon off, versus mainstream waiters, who work all day, serving food to people who get to eat it.

To say that I am irritated by this discovery is like saying the Ancient Mariner was thirsty: Food, food everywhere, nor any a bite to eat. We've passed at least thirty restaurants this morning, every single one of them open—except this one. And yet I am as far from having satiated my hunger as someone in the western hemisphere can get without starving.

But am I starving *enough* to get back in that car and try to find another acceptable restaurant, given the sound that awaits me: my two boys sitting in the backseat on either side of Jane, voraciously breast-feeding (they haven't eaten since breakfast, either) while clasping hands like two little White Panthers at a Milk Power rally? Which they've been attending since they were born . . . four and six *years* ago.

Hence, the question Jane and I debated in the car as we drove here from the previous mainstream restaurant that we were not allowed to eat in. The question was *not* should Jane be breast-feeding boys old enough to have a tree fort. It was whether she should be breast-feeding boys old enough to have a tree fort *while we are driving.* The issue was safety, in other words, not mental health—a local, organic, seasonal twist on the mainstream argument that talking on your cell phone while driving is dangerous. Only the potential dialogue here was between boys and breasts, all four of which might have been seriously injured if we'd let the boys out of their large and extra-large car seats to suckle without restraints. These were country roads. You never knew when you'd see a deer. Were I suddenly to have braked and the boys to have clenched their *teeth*, some *permanent*, who knows what could have happened to all four of them?

This raised a second question in my mind on the drive toward Blue Hill: Which sound did I prefer? My boys in the backseat screaming with hunger, or my boys in the backseat satisfying their hunger by drinking my wife? The answer, I decided, was that I preferred to hear my boys in the backseat screaming, since screaming seemed like a normal consequence of starvation, and, in any case, *normal*, versus drinking my wife, a sound that, coming out of human beings, is definitely not normal, being somewhere on the sonic spectrum between lingerie sloshing in the delicate cycle and the sucking sound as the last drops of bathtub water disappear down the drain—again and again and *again*—in stereo. (Although, in fairness to the limitations of my senses, I can never tell whether what really upsets me is listening to the little guys suckling behind me, or actually seeing them chowing down in the rearview mirror.) So I let them scream while we hurtled through the backwoods in search of a local, organic, seasonal restaurant—until we pulled up to that Victorian café in Blue Hill and parked on the side of the road. Jane got into the backseat, the boys got out of their seat belts, and I got out of the car.

Then my cell phone rings. It's my sister Kate's boyfriend, Roger. "Hello, mate." He's from Australia, so I'm his mate. Though we've never met. "I wish I had better news," he says. "If you want to say good-bye to your sister, I suggest you get on the next plane to Houston."

It's the not the first time I've heard this. Kate was diagnosed with breast cancer five years ago, and since then she and (for the last few months, since they met on the beach at a bar during happy hour) he have been calling to say her cancer has spread, then to say it has shrunk, then to say it has spread again. Resulting in everyone in my family shrinking in disbelief and spreading conspiracy theories. Like maybe the cancer is a ploy? Maybe Kate just wants *attention*?

Last year when I flew to Houston to see my mom's new face, which was her seventy-fifth-birthday present to herself (an *acceptable* way of attracting attention in my family), I met with Kate's oncologist and said, "Tell me the truth." He said, "Four years ago, I had thirty-five patients with Kate's diagnosis. Today, three of them are still alive." That was a year ago. "Your sister has inspired me to write a book," he said, "about the relationship between life expectancy and humor. Kate is *hilarious*—and I believe that's why she's still here." I reported this to my family, and we all agreed: The thirty-two patients who died of metastatic breast cancer had no sense of humor. As opposed to Kate, who was obviously sick, definitely funny, but *not* terminal—or she would have died already.

But here's Roger, who's saying she's been admitted to the critical care unit and is not expected to live. And if I want to say good-bye, "Get on the next plane . . ."

I don't want to get on the next plane—or any plane. Because as upsetting as the news is that Kate may die, even more upsetting is the possibility that I might die first, in a plane crash.

I've hated flying ever since my parents divorced when I was in kindergarten and my dad took me up one alternate weekend in the company plane. He taught me about the gauges: "This measures altitude. That measures speed." Then he shut off an engine, nodded at the sputtering propeller, pointed to the red needles in the round glass case that indicated we were losing altitude and speed, and asked me, as though *I* were the retired decorated bomber pilot and he was the kindergartner, "What do we do now, son?" To this day, my father insists this never happened. "Your mother told you that," he says—to help her win custody, in the event the judge put a kindergartner on the stand. But even if this near-death experience is imagined, the product of my mother's "scheming" instead of my father's "sense of humor," I hate flying. I already risked my life last year to see my mom's new face. I don't want to risk it again.

I call my big sister Corinne. At ten years older than I am, she's the problem solver in the family, unlike my big brother Earl, seven years older, who's a problem dodger (it runs in the male line) and Kate, five years older, who's currently the problem. Corinne lives in Houston. She can *drive* to the hospital and hopefully discover it's another false alarm and therefore I can stay here, starving on the sidewalk in Blue Hill, where I am telling my sister, "Roger says Kate is going to die."

Corinne says, "I've heard that before!"

I say, "So have I!"

She says, "I'll drive to the hospital right now!"

I say, "Good!"

She says, "Stay tuned!"

It's thrilling. We're detectives cracking a case: The Sister Who Cried Metastasized Breast Cancer Wolf. It's such a relief to be dealing with possible pathological lying rather than potential death.

I pocket the phone and get in the car, the air fragrant with fresh breast milk, which, depending on my mood, is somewhere on the olfactory spectrum between vanilla pound cake and tube socks after three sets of tennis on a summer day, and it hits me: I may never see my sister again. Because as much as I hate to fly, I *know* Roger's telling the truth.

I start the engine and drive off. A car passes us on the road—a family wagon of the kind Jane and I have debated buying, to go with our new life in the country.

Jane says, "I really like that car. What do you think?"

I say, "I don't want to talk about cars!" I've wounded her without warning. It's partly due to hunger: I have by now metabolized all my fat, and all my patience. Partly it's resentment that Jane is so strong-willed about what food our kids can eat—and I'm so weak-willed about forcing her to compromise in the face of starvation. And partly I snap because Jane's priorities seem so petty compared to my life-and-death concerns. Which Jane doesn't know about, because I haven't told her. One of the things you do after smelling breast milk on the same child for six years is defend yourself—lower the portcullis, close the gates.

One of the reasons for breast-feeding the same child for six years (and another for four) is *because* you defend yourself—lower the portcullis, close the gates. "Why should I stop doing what I think is right," says Jane, during one of our regular arguments, "if you're not . . . *here*?"

I answer the phone.

"I'm at the hospital," says Corinne, whispering, electronic beeping and metal-on-metal clanking in the background. "Kate's in intensive care."

"How is she?"

"I haven't been able to talk to her," says Corinne. "They've got her all drugged up. I'm looking at her through the window."

"*Window*?"

"I think you better get down here," says Corinne. "Maybe not right away. But . . . tomorrow?" Sugar-coating the difference between "Life as you know it is going to end tonight" versus "in the morning." Which actually does make me feel better, less urgently afraid, like there's still a chance that life and death will magically trade places. There's a reason why Corinne runs a makeup shop called Facade: She has a gift for putting the best-possible face on the worst-possible news—whether it's your looks or your sister on a ventilator.

I put the phone away, tell Jane what's happening, and stare at the road, picturing my suitcase in the trunk. I've just returned from a business trip. We're halfway to Albany. I could keep driving to the airport, buy my ticket on the way, be at Kate's bedside in a few hours. But this feels too . . . *easy*. Like God is trying to get me on the next plane out to kill me.

I should drive home, like a normal guy who thinks God is trying to kill him—someone who doesn't have his clothes with him and therefore has to go home to pack.

I'm not a normal guy. I'm a guy with a wife who, faced with two starving boys old enough to help their father build a tree fort, would rather breast-feed them than let them eat a cheese-burger. I need to get out of here. Even if it means I'm going to die today. The good news is, I won't die of hunger. They serve burgers at the airport.

TWO

Bereavement Fare

*We spent the 4ᵗʰ of July in Vermont. The fireworks
across Lake Champlain were glorious, and terrifying:
seeing the explosions before I heard them. Light travels
faster than sound. I couldn't help but think of our
marriage. What am I not hearing? What am I not
saying?*
—journal entry

I'm standing at the ticket counter in the Albany airport, alongside Jane and the boys, one straddling my shoulders, the other
holding my hand, listening to the airline agent explain the problem: My flight to Houston is delayed. I can take a later flight on
the same airline via Chicago, but I might have to stay there
overnight. Or I can switch to another airline and fly to Houston
direct, *right now.* "Which would you prefer," the agent asks me,
as though this is a rhetorical question. What normal guy *wouldn't*
want to fly direct, right now, to see his sister before she dies?

Like I'm a normal guy.

It's all I can do not to hold up a cross and stamp the agent's forehead. She thinks she's doing me a favor, not realizing (in her defense) that she is helping God try to trick me into making a little change (my airline) that will result in the big change: my death. God is like the Devil that way.

"I prefer not to change airlines," I say. "I'd rather change . . . *airports.*"

"Excuse me?" She doesn't understand that changing airports in order *not* to change airlines more closely preserves my original intention, reducing the chances that God or the Devil will notice me.

"Can you get me on a flight in the morning out of La Guardia?" I say. Which means I'd leave from New York City, 140 miles away (as the jumbo jet flies) from where we are currently standing. Granted, this is a perhaps confusing request—irrational fears are almost always confusing to a rational person. But all things considered, changing airports is less trouble than getting killed in a plane crash.

She confirms my new flight out of La Guardia, leaving tomorrow.

I grab my suitcase off the scale and lead the boys and Jane back out to the short-term-parking garage.

With the few remaining calories I have left, I drive toward the train station in Brookville, stopping off without incident at Pandemonium, an all-night Chinese fried-rice stand, where the food, I wager, contains more salt and chemicals ounce for ounce than the brackish, PCB-polluted Hudson River water presumably they use to prepare it. Their fried rice makes a Big Mac look like a vegan supercleanse. Yet here is Jane, offering no objection when I order four boxes to go.

It's hard to know what makes your wife tick sometimes, especially when you don't ask her, as intimate conversations about differences between the two of you generally turn into barbed disagreements and sometimes violent arguments, leading to suicidal and homicidal fantasies. And I don't really want to kill myself, or at least Jane, so to the degree I am able to restrain myself, I just wonder at the irritating inconsistencies in Jane's behavior, ignoring the inconsistencies in mine. Jane can worry about those.

But as with anyone, a few of Jane's inconsistencies work in my favor. And at the moment, as best as I can tell, in the rock/paper/scissors hierarchy of her local/seasonal/organic—that is, locavore—rule book, eating salt-packed fried rice is okay as long as it's local. Moreover, Pandemonium's carbon footprint (like the actual footprints of the people who work there) is probably smaller than any fast-food chain's.

Plus, Jane has a background in helping displaced, alienated, suffering workers. As someone who is half German, and grew up around the world, she relates to them, foreigner to foreigner—in this case, the Chinese living in Brookville, where the population is generally wealthy, white, homosexual weekenders or poor black locals—the twin pillars of Brookville's economy seeming to be antiques and crack cocaine. But even an antiquing sodomite or a toothless crackhead needs to eat—as do locavores and *lactivists*. ("What do we want? Breast milk! When do we want it? Now!") So we're all here at Pandemonium, where displaced, alienated, suffering Chinese workers are willing to feed us, no matter how we spent our day.

A few minutes later, after I score my pint of fried rice to go, I'm sitting on the train to New York, waving through the window to my wife and children, and then enjoying the sublime sweet-and-sour flavors of suffering and alienation, displaced onto the southbound Amtrak.

A few hours later, I'm in New York, in my office—a storage unit in our old apartment building on Central Park West—lying on my back on a camping mattress, looking up at the fiberglass-wrapped pipes dangling from the ceiling and raining little yellow specks down on me, wondering which death is worse: glass lung or (if the pipes make good on their threat and fall on my head) blunt trauma—or breast cancer? I'm counting fiberglass snow-flakes instead of sheep to put myself to sleep.

Then, I'm sitting in the back of a taxi en route to La Guardia. My driver's name is Macho, and Macho is railing against the mayor. "A billionaire who makes the little guy pay," he says. Or that's what I think he says. Macho's English is barely intelligible. Which is frustrating, especially at five in the morning, when I want to contemplate the death of my sister and/or my marriage (if I don't die first in a plane crash).

I try to change the subject from politics—which requires words—to immigration, which is basically numbers. "How long have you been here in New York?" I ask, expecting him to say, "Three weeks," or maybe "Three months."

Macho says, "Fifteen years." Or that's what I think he says.

I sit there looking out the window at the sun rising over the Triborough Bridge, stunned by how long a person can go without changing. How time can just run out. Being well brought up and a devoted father to my boys, I don't tell Macho he should do us both a favor and drive over the side of the Triborough into the East River—that both of us got stuck a long time ago, so let's just make it official and call it a life. Nor do I tell him that, like the mayor (when the mayor is not flying his private jet or helicopter), I am flying first-class. Because, in my defense, that's the only ticket there was: When you tell an airline you need to get to Houston right away to see your sister before she dies, they charge you more than you have ever been charged in your life for anything, except your apartment. It's like a prebe-reavement fare, designed to devastate you financially, so that when you are devastated emotionally sometime after arriving at your destination, it won't seem so painful. Or maybe it's just more proof that waiting till the last minute can cost you dearly.

Regardless, like so much else in this inflated world (banks where half the employees are vice presidents, Little League baseball teams that award trophies for losing), a seat in first class does not mean what it used to: I find myself eating food that I used to eat in coach, with Jane, when she ate food other people ate, before she gave birth and became enlightened: a sausage, egg, and cheese croissant for breakfast; and for lunch, a Reuben, with two free first-class beers to numb me against the turbulence—the main reason I hate flying, unlike Jane, who actually enjoys it. "It breaks up the monotony," she says. "Otherwise, it's like riding a bus."

I like riding in buses. That's why my favorite type of airplane is an Airbus. Monotony is a virtue at 35,000 feet. But not to Jane.

Or to Kate. Years ago, we were on a prop plane to Fresno, when it hit some chop (as pilots like to euphemize turbulence) and we began bobbing, and, in my case, sobbing—inside. Kate was in the seat in front of me—we were sitting single file. I was crushing my armrests with terror, literally white-knuckled, when Kate turned around with a smile on her face, like she looked when we rode the Matterhorn together as children at Disneyland, after my father had tricked me into riding with him, even though I was below the minimum age—before tricking the attendant into letting me ride. "Don't worry, Hunt," Kate said, using my middle name, her nickname for me. "I know I'm not going to die in a plane crash. God has bigger plans for me."

Sitting on the aisle now, in A2, I'm realizing Kate was right.

Then Alicia, who is sitting in A1, asks me to switch seats with her husband, who is sitting in A4, across the aisle.

"No, sorry," I say.

"You don't like window seats, huh?"

"I like 'em fine," I say. They allow me to talk to the ground much more easily than from an aisle seat. And unlike my driver Macho, the ground can talk back in a language I can understand. And since the ground is solid, if we're talking, the ground and I, I'll be solid, too. None of which I tell Alicia. "I just don't like to change things once I sit down," I say. "Because if I move . . . the plane might crash." I stop short of telling her how I know this—that I know nothing about how planes work, but I know how God works: Little changes add up to the big change—and none of us wants *that*. Because, unlike Kate, I have not been told by God that I will not die in a plane crash. On the contrary.

"You sat next to the right person," says Alicia. "My husband is a pilot."

"My dad was a pilot," I say.

"My dad was a pilot, too!" says Alicia.

Clearly, our dads were cut from different piloting cloth. Hers did not cut power to the engines.

I say, "You married your father."

She says, "When you put it like that, yeah, I guess so." It's as though it never occurred to her that perhaps it's more than coincidence her father and her husband both love flying—any more than it occurred to me that perhaps it's more than coincidence my sister and my wife are really comfortable with turbulence.

THREE

The Devils You Know

I am drawn to you
Like the river to the sea
What becomes of the freshwater fish?
—poem for Jane, year one

I met Jane at the Hungarian Pastry Shop, a little café a few blocks down from Columbia University. I was a student at the time, writing a poem to Anna, my current ex-girlfriend. It was called "The Devils You Know," and I had just written:

You remind me of my big sister
Who reminds me of my mom

Then I heard a voice.

"Look at him. Isn't he classic? He thinks he's writing the great American novel."

I looked up to strike back but was smitten into silence by a remarkable pair of legs sheathed in black spandex attached to a ski-sweatered torso, all belonging to a striking woman in her middle twenties with radiant blue eyes and luxurious swept-back dirty-blonde hair, like Ingrid Bergman, had Ingrid Bergman been a grad student, or Beethoven, had Beethoven been a beautiful woman in alpine ski clothing.

Whereupon I picked up where I had left off, putting my rage on the page:

What a pity
None of us ever got along

I put down my pen and reached for a celebratory cigarette—everyone smoked in those days, indoors and out. My pack was spent. I'd been so drugged by anger that I'd forgotten about nicotine!

This was no time for withdrawal. I started going from table to table in a drug-addled circle, like a slow-moving lazy Susan, asking other students if they could spare a smoke.

They were out, too.

Until I get to . . .

Her! The last person in the Hungarian Pastry Shop I want to ask for a favor; somehow I didn't see her in the corner of my eye, my desperation for a cigarette having obscured my peripheral vision.

Upon closer inspection, I can see quite clearly that in addition to her fabulous legs and sparkling smile, she has a crisp pack of cigarettes on her table. And after doing the math—What is more valuable, getting drugs or sacrificing your pride by getting drugs from the woman who just insulted you?—I figure it's a no-brainer. "Could you spare a cigarette?"

"I'll give you a cigarette," she says. "If you give me a copy of your poem when it's published."

It would be cool to impersonate a writer, it seems to me, when the truth is that I am a marginally functional undergraduate with notebooks full of unpublished poems. But if I lie to her and she finds out, that'll be the end of whatever sex I might be able to squeeze out of this pastry shop connection. Poetic justice indeed.

"I'm just a student," I say.

"Then let me read it now."

A hate poem is generally not an aphrodisiac, not what you use to attract a beautiful woman—whether or not she has insulted you. Even I know that. But I need to smoke.

I give her my notebook.

She gives me a cigarette.

She starts reading.

I light up.

Then she takes out a red pen and starts correcting.

"What are you *doing*?"

"I used to be an editor," she says. "At Harvard. *Pity,* I think, is a confusing word choice. It's a little . . . sarcastic."

"It's a first draft," I say, grabbing my notebook.

"I'm not finished," she says, grabbing it back, pulling me closer, smiling that smile. It's the most irritating, irresistible thing a woman has ever done to me. *Correcting* my poem. But correcting *my* poem. Taking it seriously. Helping me communicate how bad I feel. Which makes me feel good. She's just like my poem!

So we start talking in that hyperactive, hypercompetitive way that students at hypercompetitive universities often do.

"I grew up all over the world," she says. "I speak five languages. I went to Smith, Harvard, Columbia, and now Union Seminary . . . all on scholarships. How about you?"

I could tell her I graduated with a class ranking of fifty-one . . . out of fifty-two students. After five years, instead of four. But I'm thinking the person I want to be is more attractive.

"I grew up in the *West*," I say, trying to evoke images of wild horses and wide-open spaces instead of used cars and strip malls. "Came east to be a songwriter, yeah. But I'm an English major. *For now.* 'Cause I love Shakespeare almost as much as I love the Beatles."

"You write songs? I could never do that. My mother is an English professor, and when I brought home my first A paper from Smith—on *Emma*—she said it should have been a B. So I switched majors from English to political science, so she couldn't understand me."

"I guess I'm lucky," I say. "My mom has never read a word I've written." Not a bad thing when you're writing "The Devils You Know."

"That's a shame," she says, smiling.

I could talk to her forever. I know it. But she's here with a friend, who's just staring at us, awkwardly—a highly visible yet silent fifth wheel. It's starting to feel weird.

"Maybe we could do this another time?" she says.

"I'd like that," I say, ripping off the bottom of "The Devils You Know," holding my pen at the ready.

"I'm Jane."

I start writing J-A-N-E, slowly and carefully, in big block letters, so there won't be any mistakes, like this is the winning ticket to emotional (and sexual) lotto, so that even if the rain washes off the ink on the walk home, I'll still see the impression of the letters.

Then Jane grabs *that* out of my hand. "I hate to see my name in big block letters," she says, finishing in flowing cursive, adding her number, and handing it back.

That night, I'm lying in bed, reading the scrap of paper like it's a poem: JANE . . . JANE . . . JANE . . . over and over.

I love her name.

I love her handwriting.

I hate how it got on this paper.

I put the scrap on the bedside table, propping it up on its side, and stare at it, as though Jane were lying next to me.

Then I lean over and kiss the paper good night as I turn out the light.

How long should I wait to call? I wonder when I wake up the next morning. I don't want Jane to think I'm desperate.

But I *am* desperate.

But desperation is not an aphrodisiac, any more than a hate poem is. But she *liked* my hate poem. What do I know?

I decide to wait three days, as though I'm busy. I read somewhere that this is the appropriate amount of time to simulate having a real life—that is, interests that precede and supersede a man's interest in a woman. In other words, being busy is an aphrodisiac.

Three nights later, I'm standing at a pay phone on Broadway and 112th Street. In goes the dime. Around goes the dial. Jane's busy, too; no call waiting. Who's she talking to? I wonder. Why hasn't she forsaken all other interests and friendships to make herself available for me, just as I have for her? She told me she would be busy each night till nine—and to call her then. Which I'm trying to do. As she asked me to. But she didn't say that her *phone* would be busy. I can't get through, even after an hour of trying.

She must be talking to her girlfriend. About me. It makes me smile through the anxiety and the fear and the disappointment as I walk away from the phone booth, the thought of being talked about by *two* girls. The object of their desires: "I want James!" The subject of their fears: "Does he like me?" Like giddy girlfriends on the playground, or in the stands at a lacrosse game, whispering about the stud. Like a verbal ménage a trois. The two of them concerned only with my needs. Screw reality! It's comforting being comfortable being self-absorbed.

I slip the scrap with Jane's number back into my wallet and amble back home.

The next night at 9:00 P.M., I call her again. Busy again—for an hour.

And again, the night after that. Which is when I realize that Jane is not talking to her girlfriend about me. She is talking to the new boyfriend who openly pursued her while I waited to call her in my dorm room for three days, simulating having a real life.

Which is the moment—had I the ability to observe aberrant behaviors in myself versus just in the mice in the Skinner box experiments that I perform in the cognitive-psychology lab on Tuesday and Thursday afternoons—that I begin behaving like a psychotic lab mouse. Only, I am more desperate than a lab mouse, my dime-slotting worse than a mouse's fruitless attempts to press a lever and get food. But, as I am a psychotic man, not a mouse, I have streamlined the process like a human systems engineer.

Step 1: Telephone headset is cradled between right ear and shoulder, my dominant side, freeing both hands.

Step 2: Left hand holds the scrap of paper with Jane's number.

Step 3: Right hand deposits the dime, then returns to the dial, index finger hovering over the number holes, poised for action as . . .

Step 4: Count to one (silently) while the dime falls through the mechanism, registers, and I hear the dial tone.

Step 5: Insert right index finger into the first number hole and rotate dial; then remove tip of finger and poise it over the next number hole while the dial returns to its starting position.

Step 6: Alternate left and right fingertips throughout the seven-number sequence to minimize fingertip abrasion.

Step 7: After dialing the seventh number, poise the right— that is, more dexterous—fingertip outside the coin-return slot.

Step 8: When the busy signal sounds, depress the switch hook with the left finger, wait for the dime to drop down into the coin-return slot, insert the right fingertip and remove the coin by flicking it out onto the left palm.

Step 9: Grab the coin with the right hand and repeat.

Step 10: Vary this routine only to (a) let dimes accumulate in the coin-return slot so as to rest right fingertip or (b) slam the receiver down on the switch hook instead of pressing it with the finger so as to feel and hear the satisfying crash of plastic into metal and thereby vent rage and fear and despair that the woman I am sure will change my life has slipped away from me because I did not know how to show her I wanted her before somebody else did.

Every night.

For three weeks.

Then I return to my dorm room, take the scrap of paper with Jane's number out of my wallet, place it on my bedside table, look at it one last time—*so close and yet so far away*—then flick it over the side and watch it float down into the wastebasket, the paper almost translucent and soft as a chamois from all the ins and outs to and from my wallet. Granted, I rarely empty my wastebasket; like a lot of students, hygiene and housework are not my favorite subjects. But there's a chance—in my jealousy-addled, terror-rattled, magical-thinking brain—that a housekeeper will magically appear and take my trash away, and with it my connection to Jane.

In the meantime, there it lies: used tissues and empty yogurt containers and candy wrappers and wadded early drafts of poems and songs—along with a little scrap of paper with a four-letter, seven-number combination that I thought would unlock me from despair but, at the moment, is breaking my heart.

FOUR

Dating Up

People are like dogs, son.
You can wish you were a German Shepherd
all day long.
But if you were born a poodle, you'll die a poodle.
—my father

I'm sitting at a mahogany table in the cavernous Reading Room of Butler Library one night, right in the middle of campus, studying for midterms. Butler is a grand, high-ceilinged place, with books stacked and scattered in front of each student, so just sitting there makes you feel *normal,* like you are more than a student torturing lab mice on Tuesdays and Thursdays by withholding food from them unless they stumble upon the random, no-discernible-pattern pattern (which they never will discern!) that will unlock the food from the lever-triggered dispenser that they can see and smell but cannot access—a so-close-yet-so-far-away proximity that is slowly driving them insane; while majoring in English and philosophy, which has yielded, among other pearls, that Nietzsche was a virgin until he broke his vow of chastity with a prostitute who gave him syphilis—in the time before antibiotics, which meant a death sentence—after inexorably rotting his body and his brain, but not before he hatched the bon mot "What does not kill me makes me stronger." Until it killed him.

My friend Fred sits down at my mahogany table. Fred used to be an actor on a soap opera, until he realized his mother was right: One day his matinee-idol (technically, soap-opera-star) good looks would fade and he'd need a plan B. So he returned to college to get a degree and maybe become a real estate broker, or some kind of businessman. In any case, he dresses for success—camel's hair coat, deep blue cashmere scarf, Positano Sun Center tan, perfectly coifed, if oddly tinted, blond hair—he's a paragon of personal grooming. The only thing out of place is that Fred does not have any books with him—evidently he's already studied, or perhaps he's come to check a book out. Either way, he's buzzing with excitement.

"I met the most amazing woman today!" he says with a kind of heterosexual enthusiasm one normally associates with a heterosexual, versus Fred, who is gay. "I had sexual feelings for her! I think my mom was right! I think I may be straight!" Unlike my other gay friends, Fred looks and acts straight—essential for his success as a romantic lead on a soap opera. He's the Rock Hudson of the daytime drama set; you don't get cast as a leading man if the audience thinks you want to bed the other leading man. Plus, his mom wants him to bring home a girlfriend for Christmas. So this is *huge*.

"Oh my God!" I say, with—I like to think—no judgment, just amazement. I have no stake Fred's sexual orientation, but I do have a vested interest in the possibility of wholesale change. When I'm not torturing mice, I'm reading Shakespeare, especially the comedies, and I've come to believe in the Shakespearean forest— the notion that you can enter into a wood troubled, haunted, desperate, then emerge with the crown rightfully restored to your weary head, even if you weren't a king and had no crown to begin with. "That's incredible!" I say, feeling joy at Fred's joy, inspired by his transformation.

"*She's* incredible!" says Fred. "She lived all over the world. Speaks five languages. Went to Harvard. Has *amazing* legs. She's more exciting than a guy!"

"That sounds like the woman I just met," I say, as though it's a coincidence, an idle fact, concealing terror and fear of having suddenly detected a rival behind the calm dissimulation I've learned from a lifetime of killing inferior creatures. I look at Fred the way I look at a lab mouse, or a mosquito on my arm, until . . . *splat.* He can't know I know he's there, until it's too late. You might call what I'm doing acting, just as Fred acts like he's my straight friend, instead of a homosexual vaporizing what little heterosexual confidence I have left. All the world really is a stage I gather up my books, slip on my coat, and prepare to bolt. It's bad enough to lose a woman to a man, but to a gay man? Screw Shakespeare—some wounds cannot be healed. If I can't beat Fred for Jane's affections, I might as well climb to the top of my dorm and jump. Students commit suicide here all the time for a lot less than this. "Was her name Jane?" I say.

"Yes!" says Fred.

"Was her last name . . . Amsterdam?"

"I don't know!" says Fred. "She didn't tell me her last name."

"She told me. And she gave me her number. I'll see you later!"

SPLAT! It's a sickening feeling, watching a would-be-straight man's face transform back to gay in real time, right in front of you. And yet it's so charmingly naïve and innocent for a man to think that his battle for sexual gratification is within himself: Am I straight or am I gay? Like *that* matters. Versus the reality: Is she more attracted to me than she is to him—my rival for her affections? And the body that goes with them? Fred, regardless of his sexual disorientation, is now in competition with every other straight man on a campus with twenty thousand students, including me and—this being New York City—thousands of lesbians: Barnard, the women's college, is right across the street! And some of those girls are hot! Who knows if Jane is *experimenting*? Many women here do. But Fred doesn't realize that he has entered a new world; doesn't see that he has left behind a takes-one-to-know-one old world of monosexuality, where he understood the rules from the inside out, where he was both predator and prey and therefore assured of constant satisfaction, from above or below the food chain, and is now a hunter in a bifurcated world of tremendous scarcity, where many predators starve, alone in their dorm rooms, reading *Playboy* and Penguin classics. *Welcome to the jungle!*

Whatever chemical it is that your body releases to neutralize joy and compassion for a friend and replace it with homicidal jealousy and suicidal fear and abject terror and the kind of hunger and thirst from spending forty days and forty nights in the desert knowing I will die if I don't win the battle for your sexual favors, that's what propels me out of my seat and out of the library at what I hope is under the speed limit over which the security guard will force me to stop!

Until I get to the front door and bolt across campus, like the thieves you see running down the sidewalk holding bouquets of roses they've stolen from Korean delis.

Into my dorm building.

Up the stairs.

Into my room, where—thank God I am a magical thinker, but the world is not magical and the imaginary housekeeper has not come and emptied my real trash—I rescue the worn scrap of paper from my wastebasket and secure it in my wallet.

Run back down the stairs.

Across the street.

Through the wrought-iron campus gates, to the student center, where (thanks, to the student who mans the information desk at night) I change a ten-dollar bill into a roll of quarters.

Over to the phone booth—an old romantic wooden box with a seat and a door, which I close.

I sit down and take out Jane's number and place it on the little shelf under the phone, along with the quarters. I take out a coin, and after I've stopped hyperventilating, I dial. For the first time, I hear a *ring*. I'm finally in her bedroom.

The ringing stops. "Hello?"

How little it takes to change your life when your life is teetering and fragile. Just the sound of her voice fills me with hope and purpose. I say, in my bedroom voice, "Jane?"

She says, "Who *is* this?" Like I'm stalking her. Which I am.

"James?" Nothing. "From the Hungarian Pastry Shop?" Nothing. "You corrected my poem?"

"Oh," she says, cutting me off mid-humiliation. "I almost forgot about you. What took you so long?"

"It's not easy getting through."

"Well, here I am."

"Right. Now that I found you, let's go out . . . for coffee."

"Now?"

"Yes."

"I'm in my nightgown."

"Well take it off . . . and put on some clothes."

"I don't want to take it off. That's why I put it on."

"What are you, fifty?"

"You are so aggressive."

"Really? *I'm* aggressive?" I say, just to confirm the good news. Nobody's called me aggressive since freshman year, when I got an A in photography for having the boldness to photograph pot dealers in Washington Square.

"It's late," she says. "But we can talk. If you like."

An hour and a roll of quarters later, I'm still on the phone with a Smith, Harvard, Columbia, Union scholarship student.

Who thinks I'm a peer. Who thinks I belong.

I am a peer. I do belong. I'm more than I've ever been.

As long as we keep talking.

FIVE

The Predator's Disco Ball

I don't want to know your last name. I don't want to know anything about you. Let's just enjoy each other. Like that movie where the guy follows the woman around to art galleries and doesn't ask questions. I'm going to marry a European noble. But if I still like you, maybe you can be my lover! I just never pictured myself with an American, especially one from Texas.
—Jane, year one

During our first telephone conversation, Jane suggested that I meet her at the next gay and lesbian dance, which is held on campus once a month. This being New York City, there are lots of gays and lesbians on campus, and given that many have relocated here primarily to *be* gay and lesbian without fear of violent reprisal, the gay and lesbian dances are exuberant affairs, living testaments to what one of Jane's Old Testament professors might have observed is proof that the spirit of Sodom and Gomorrah is alive and well and copulating in and about the juniper bushes of Earl Hall on 118th and Broadway.

Jane was going to be at the dance anyway, she said. For my part, I'd been curious to see what really happened inside (and outside) of Earl Hall, as I have always been drawn to people who've lived in fear of getting harmed by their families.

So here I am at the dance, dressed like a soldier in camouflage (the better to blend in)—green worsted-wool suit with a skinny black tie—standing in the shadows of a dark, triple-height-ceilinged, disco-balled, gloriously beautiful Stanford White–designed formal hall full of homosexual undergraduates, watching at arm's length as they pulse with the knowledge that they are going to have sex with one another later tonight (or maybe sooner) and not get crucified for it as they had been back home.

Then I see Jane, dancing in the center of it all with what I hope is a homosexual, the way he preens his sunken chest and shimmies his slender hips and thrusts his little (hopefully) gay pelvis out at Jane. Then he suddenly unfurls his serpentine tongue, in an image reminiscent of the famous picture of Elvis Presley touching his tongue tip to the lips of an unidentified besotted female admirer. Only in this case, the female admirer is Jane! I am watching a man (I guess he's not homosexual) kiss the woman I am going to spend the rest of my life with before *I* get to kiss her! Which, on the spectrum of heart-piercing acts of cuckoldry, may be even more extreme than watching a man kiss her *after*!

When Jane sees me standing in the circle of bodies surrounding the dance floor, she dances over and says, "You made it!"

"I told you I would," I say cooly, shocked and enraged and jealous at the tongue-washing I've just witnessed gay Elvis giving her—and her utter guilelessness in the (wet) face of it all. Doesn't she know she's *mine*? That those *seemingly* crazy Muslim fundamentalists who sacked the United States Embassy in Iran so they could cover up their women in chadors are really just taking the heat for the *seemingly* enlightened rest of us? Seriously, who do you think of when you think of chastity belts? Muhammad, or King Arthur?

"I'm glad you're here," says Jane—screams Jane really— through the disco din.

"I am, too," I say. Like there had been a possibility that I would not be here.

"This is Christopher," she says, introducing gay Elvis, as though I want to know his name. As though I want anything more than to forget what I've just seen: a kiss from a tongue as long as Gene Simmons's, the front man of the rock band Kiss, whose legendarily long tongue supposedly is the product of surgical enlargement. Far from wanting to meet my competition, I want nothing more than to wash my memory (and Jane's face) clean of this homo hyperlong-lingual-lapper Kiss kisser violating my pristine possession. Whom, I know, I should not treat like a possession, as she is not mine—*yet*. Plus, there is something to be said for faking heterosexual confidence in the face of a gay predator. After all, it worked with Fred in the library.

Why do gay men like her anyway? Because she's a diva? Sure of herself? Someone who corrects not only your poem on the day you meet but your actual handwriting as you write her name on a little scrap of paper that she grabs out of your hand? Because she's emasculating? To a straight man anyway. But beside the point to a homosexual; his emasculatables never enter into the equation.

I do not know what attracts men like Christopher to Jane. I know only that I've seen enough, and that I need to forgive Jane for publicly semicuckolding her future husband with a homosexual—the way a gay man would forgive her, and unlike a fundamentalist Muslim, who is so terrified of female sexuality that he ends up so sexually frustrated he is willing to kill himself to get to heaven early to have sex with a virgin. Which I totally understand. Except I want that virgin here and now, on Earth. (Holiday Christians are really philistines that way, as are atheists.) I am going to make believe that I didn't just see *my* virgin kissing a gay man and that she is, was, and always will be mine, mine, *mine*!

I walk her back from the dance and stand outside the entrance to her dorm. She can't find her keys. The work-study student and so-called security guard has left his post. I circle the building, looking for an open window. When I return from my dash around the city block to report the mixed blessing that all the street-level windows of the seminary are locked and we can't break in, Jane thanks me for trying, tells me the security guard has returned, and leans in and kisses me good night.

"I'm not afraid to be aggressive," she says.

I kiss her back. "I'm not afraid, either," I say, as though who kissed whom is a competition.

Before saying good night, we confirm our first official date: a Halloween party full of seminarians. Believers. Whom Jane has led me to believe are not at all like fundamentalists—Christian or Muslim. But more like Christopher, the preening, prancing, tongue dancer whose kiss I had just replaced with my own, in my own little version of a wild alpha-stallion mustang kicking the side of his just-mated-with-a-beta-stallion mustang mare to force a spontaneous abortion before he mounts her—only a little less aggressive. More like a dog spraying a tree a few minutes after the previous dog sprayed it, only a little more attractive. More like a marginally functional undergraduate trying to woo a lovely scholarship student who is three years older and four institutions of higher learning more advanced away from her mystifying attraction to her homosexual admirer (who, while homosexual, is a much better dancer and has a much longer tongue) and replace her feelings for him with an equally mystifying and no less real attraction to me.

SIX

The Bride of Christ

You will never bore me. I know you'll grow and change.
That we can be different things to each other.
Because I know I'm going to change. A lot.
—Jane, year one

Jane's dorm is on 122nd and Broadway, so I meet her downstairs at the guard desk, kiss her on the cheek, lead her outside, and hail a cab.

It's a brawny act for a scrawny undergraduate—lifting my arm to hail a taxi. I was born in Texas, and grew up in Denver, and in Denver you don't lift your arm except to spray deodorant. And you *never* hail a taxi. You open the Yellow Pages and *call* a taxi, or you stand in a line at the airport and *wait* for a taxi—if you're so impoverished that you can't afford your own car. In Denver, taxis are for losers. And even if they're not for losers, raising my arm on the street feels uncomfortable—like, I *want* this. Like, I am not going to wait three days to call you. I want you *now*. It's just so damned bold. And I'm not bold. I'm Denver. And what if my deodorant's not working?

But my arm's up, the taxi slows down, and I'm in charge.

Jane says, "What are you doing?"

I say, "Hailing a taxi," as though it's not obvious.

Jane says, "Let's take a bus. It's cheaper."

I say, "I'm paying." As I've been raised to do.

My first date was in the ninth grade, with a girl named Sherry. She sat next to me in typing class, in the back corner of the room, which gave me a little unsupervised two-desk cocoon in which to court her. After a few weeks of hunting and pecking, I banged out a little note, asking Sherry if she wanted to have a date. I didn't know what that meant; I just knew people did it, and that I was a person.

When I told my brother, Earl, about this, he arranged everything: He drove me to the wine shop and bought a bottle of something called Château Lafite Rothschild; he hired our housekeeper, Edith, to pour the wine, and cook and serve the New York strip steaks and baked potatoes; and (after letting me try to use my learner's permit to drive the Cadillac over to Sherry's house, before I drove off the road in the dark and nearly into the ditch and he changed seats with me) he personally chauffeured me back and forth to Sherry's, while Sherry and I sat in the backseat. Sherry complained that the Château Lafite Rothschild was too sour, and asked for Welch's grape juice instead, which Edith gamely decanted into the crystal goblets. But apart from that, the evening went off without a hitch. Earl had wooed a French baron's daughter, and my father had married relatively wealthier women two times at this point, partly on the strength of their gallantry; who was I to second-guess what it meant in my family to be a man?

Jane, on the other hand, has no qualms about second-guessing me. "Whatever you pay," she says, "I'll have to pay on the way back. And I can't afford a cab."

"But I don't want you to pay on the way back. I'll pay for both ways."

"Then pay for my token."

Pretty soon, my arm is up again, holding the bar in the back of a bus rumbling down Broadway, my attempt to take charge having once again been thwarted. The good news is that I have about ten more dollars in my wallet than I'd planned on having— money I really wanted to spend on Jane. It's just like the moment I heard Jane's voice for the first time in the pastry shop, the moment I saw her correcting my poem, our first conversation: I'm seething and smitten, at once. Déjà vu all over again.

I don't know what I was expecting to see at a Halloween party full of seminarians, but I wasn't expecting to see the Bride of Christ—much less the transvestite Bride of Christ. But here she is, standing in an apartment in a wedding dress, a crown of thorns atop a wig under a lace veil, with bloody stigmata on her hairy hands and hairy sandaled feet—and (in homage to doubting Thomas) a spear-shaped tear and a bloody stain on her abdomen.

Which might be amusingly odd, archly perverted, or just benignly weird—if the Bride of Christ were anyone but Christopher, the flamboyant long-tongued preacher creature. Gay Elvis strikes again!

Jane is *delighted,* like a little girl clapping her hands at a magic trick. She thinks his costume is *"creative,"* unlike my costume: *not* creative—that is, clothes, which I was wearing perhaps not this afternoon, as I have dressed for a date, but which I have worn many other times. A costume no less creative than Jane's, granted—she's dressed for a date, too. But she's a woman. Everyone would rather see her out of her clothes anyway. Jane is looking at Christopher, not at me, on what's supposed to be our first date. To wear the pants with this woman, you have to wear the dress.

Life was so much easier a few weeks ago, when I was sitting in a café writing hate poems about my current old girlfriend, Anna, a dark-haired beauty who left me for art school, inanimate objects being more appealing to her than I was, not worrying about defending my new girlfriend (who doesn't know she's my new girlfriend) from the advances of a homosexual transvestite predator. It's *exhausting*, like living in the ocean: The threat could come from anywhere—above, below, in front, behind, left, right. So you grow legs and climb out of the water to live on dry land. And just when you think you're safe, here comes a homosexual transvestite to stick his tongue in your girlfriend's mouth.

The only oddly saving grace is that Christopher is dressed like a bride and not a groom. His big feet and bony hands may be coated in fake blood and mottled hair, but the hem of his gown is all pumpkin and spice. I find myself relating to him as I would to a girl, wanting to impress him, in the way that God makes any marginally functional male student want to impress anyone wearing a dress, because it triggers a lizard brain drive to impress the first wearer of a dress, the first wearer of an apron, who evidently never cut the strings. I'm a sophomore in college. It wasn't that long ago I was reading *Are You My Mother?*

Christopher says, "God, it's hot." And he peels off his veil and crown of thorns and wig to let some air in, revealing—to my mind's eye—that I've been trying to impress—flirting with—a sweaty, hairy-handed, hairy-footed, balding homosexual in a wedding dress, with a long tongue that, at least one time, has been inserted into the mouth of my (she doesn't know she's my) girlfriend, and that, presumably, wants to find its way into my mouth, too.

Which just goes to show you, ministers come in all shapes and sizes. This guy is going to graduate with an M.Div., a master's of divinity, and eventually counsel members of his flock in their times of need. Just as Jane will. After she finishes reading the memoirs of the saints. *Hildegarde of Bingen?* There could come a day when a troubled undergraduate tells him, or her, I was at a Halloween party one night with a transvestite Bride of Christ who tongued my (didn't know she was my) girlfriend . . . and Christopher (or Jane) will know how to help.

It's humbling, when I think of it. I really don't know anything.

When the party ends, we share a big Checker cab back to the seminary, Jane and I and a few other seminarians and Christopher, which allows us to split the fair for the price of a bus ride each.

Back in the dorm, Christopher asks if we'd like to have a nightcap in his room. Something about the words *nightcap* and *room* don't go together, like a bald man in a wedding gown. As the *Sesame Street* jingle put it, "One of these things is not like the others/One of these things doesn't belong . . ." which I listened to not that long ago. But when delivered with confidence by a bald man in a wedding gown, anything goes, as Cole Porter (a gay man's gay man) sang.

Soon we're sitting in Christopher's room, in a little circle of wooden school chairs, having a nightcap: red wine, vodka, a few bong hits. I've never seen dope next to a Bible before. It's a little scary, and confusing; where is the line between not-that-religious and sacrilegious? Especially if the person drawing that line is supposedly more religious than you are? If I had known this is what it meant to be a Christian, I could have been an altar boy.

Christopher proposes we do a reading of his new play. He is a playwright, evidently, and an actor, in addition to being a theater director, poet, Old Testament scholar, future minister, and all-around creative, charismatic bon vivant—a package of personality traits that together seems to neutralize the off-putting implications of his flamboyant homosexuality in the mind of my (doesn't know she's my) heterosexual girlfriend. Jane is, once again, delighted.

Christopher opens a desk drawer and pulls out a stack of pristine manuscripts bound in blue paper, with gold tacks fixed through the punch holes, and we pass them around the circle. The play is set in a monastery, Christopher explains, and it's about an older monk who, unlike the other celibate monks, secretly wants to have unholy relations with the new young monk, the monk hunk, who secretly feels the same way about the older monk, putting both monks in a struggle of faith versus the flesh. It's an amusing predicament at one in the morning on Halloween night in a seminary, all the more so when you are drunk and/or stoned.

Christopher casts the various roles and we begin reading, and the young blond seminarian whom Christopher has cast as the monk hunk reads the line about how being celibate in a monastery makes him feel like a lonely grasshopper on a twig at night and he wants to rub his hind legs against the older monk's hind legs until both sets of legs vibrate together and make fragrant music in the night air. Christopher, having cast himself as the older monk, looks into the young monk hunk's eyes and says he wants to rub his hind legs together, too. It's a very poetic image, it seems to me, and very moving as Christopher reads it; kind of like *Death in Venice* meets Mutual of Omaha's *Wild Kingdom*—thwarted, decaying homosexual impulses crossed with the dangers of the animal world mixed in with a bit of St. Augustine's *Confessions* as dramatized by Oscar Wilde.

All eyes turn to the monk hunk, a square-jawed, clean-cut blond kid from Iowa who appears to be either homosexual or an Eagle Scout, or both, to see if he'll follow the stage direction: (*They kiss*). It's a truly dramatic "Will he or won't he?" moment.

The monk hunk says, "I should get to bed." Which is not in the script.

Christopher says, "My thoughts exactly."

The other seminarians laugh.

And the monk hunk stands up and walks out—evidently having chosen to attend seminary to learn more about faith than the pleasures of fornicating with the Bride of Christ.

There's a slight pall in the room as we try to shake off the fact that Christopher has both preyed on this kid and then humiliated him for not succumbing, while the rest of us watched in amusement. So Christopher deftly, quickly neutralizes the acid by naming the monk hunk's understudy: "James."

Surprisingly, this feels like an honor—that Christopher has confidence in my ability to play the part of a homosexual monk hunk, the love interest, really, an important part of any story. I compliment him on his poetic allusions, poet-to-poet, on how he has contained, within a single metaphor, celibacy, homosexuality, and grasshoppers, and then decline. "I'm not much of an actor," I say. "Thanks anyway."

Jane hops on my lap, facing sideways, like Lady Godiva riding sidesaddle.

Christopher says, "She likes you."

Jane smiles.

I just take her in, not knowing where to put my hands. Leave them hanging down by my sides . . . simian, detached? Around her waist? Rest them on her thighs? Should I relax my hands, so she feels my weight? Move them? Or at least *animate* them, so she knows I am here, touching her? So she knows that I *like* touching her? That might remind her she's jumped on my lap! (A lot of women might consider jumping on a man's lap an error in judgment or a lapse in decorum, which, when their action is pointed out to them, they will undo by jumping back down.)

I split the difference, resting my hands on Jane's thighs, but with a reverential pressure, as I would rest my hands on the back of a church pew, holding some tension in my arms while relaxing lightly, so that she knows I am here, as I feel her weight and her volume atop me. It occurs to me that she weighs too much for me to lift, to hoist, that I am not strong enough to do all those things the porn stars do. But since we are in a seminary, in a room full of ministers in training, the missionary position seems appropriate.

Christopher may have more plays and poems and charisma than I do. But I have Jane on my lap. And right now, she feels like the world.

SEVEN

The Importance of Being Burnished

Everyone's great when the world goes their way.
The measure of insanity is, what do you do
when you don't get your way?
—my mom

I'm standing outside the front door of an apartment in Greenwich Village, holding a manila envelope full of poems I've written about Jane, waiting for Christopher to open up the door and bless them.

Like Jane, Christopher is studying in the seminary to be a master of divinity. He is also at least seven years older than I am, years during which he's done things I've only dreamed of doing: published poetry; written, directed, and acted in plays—albeit about topics I haven't dreamed of; for example, flamboyantly gay seminarians lusting after heterosexual seminarians (his plays are autobiographical), as well as things I hope never to do: get divorced and turn gay—or (even worse) vice versa; and actually read the Great Books, not just the Cliffs Notes. Passages from the Bible or Oscar Wilde tumble out of Christopher the way jokes come out of a normal guy. Which makes him both learned and tremendously irritating—because Jane admires him and values his attention.

Just as Christopher admires Jane and values her attention.

Just as I admire and value the attention of them both.

When Christopher suggested we three meet downtown for dinner at a friend's apartment—he's house-sitting while his friend is on vacation—and that I come early to discuss my writing, I was thrilled. He'd tell me I'm great, I'd tell him he's great, we'd tell Jane she's great, and we'd all have a great time. An attention ménage à trois.

I'm knocking at Christopher's front door, my poems under one arm, two bottles of white wine in my other hand, waiting for the attention to begin.

The door cracks open, seemingly of its own volition, slowly revealing a dark room full of burning candles of different lengths and shapes, some new, some old, all impaled on wrought-iron Gothic candelabra—like the scene in *The Omen* when the guy gets killed by the Devil. Which to some people would be a sign to run. But not to the guy in *The Omen*—or to me. The night I met Jane, I discovered that I was willing to risk my emotional— and perhaps even physical—life for attention.

Suddenly, dramatically, Christopher steps onto the threshold, dressed for a crucifixion in a Calvary costume, only flamboyantly gay. He's wearing a creamy silk kimono open to his emaciated belly, with a little trail of belly hair leading down and disappearing into his matching creamy briefs. He looks like Jesus, only with short, thinning hair, owlish glasses, and a mien that suggests he'll be looking down from the cross at some man, rather than at Mary Magdalene.

"Welcome," he says, sounding vaguely Transylvanian, scanning my face for a reaction.

"Hi!" I say brightly, as though this is normal. Because I grew up in a world where, when a door opened, you might see people without *any* clothes on—fornicating, injecting heroin, or, in more industrious moments, compressing dried hemp leaves into kilo bricks of fake marijuana for sale at the local park. (We were nymphomaniacs, junkies, and frauds, not drug dealers.) I don't surprise easily. If anyone is going to get attention tonight, it's going to be me.

I hand Christopher the two bottles of Chardonnay he asked me to bring, then follow him into the living room, heading toward the wineglasses on the coffee table and the dark velvet love seat, Christopher sashaying barefoot through the maze of candlelight.

The love seat looks too small to hold both me and a man in his underwear, and the chair across the room is too far away to discuss my poems. It's an either/or situation, with no middle ground; an Old Testament living room: no purgatory. So when Christopher plops down on the love seat, curls his bare feet under his Jesus briefs, and pats the cushion next to him, beckoning me to sit (a gesture I've never seen a grown man make, except to a dog or cat), I sit next to him and place my manila folder of poems on the velvet strip that separates my jeans from Christopher's bony white legs, like a barricade—and a bridge. This is why I'm here an hour early.

I've never been alone with Christopher, much less alone in the dark. So I don't know what to say to him. Mainly, what binds us is our shared admiration of Jane.

"Jane's the most amazing woman I've ever met," says Christopher, pouring the wine and breaking the ice with a familiar refrain. "You're a lucky man."

"I know. That's why I wrote these," I say, vibrating my sheath of poems between us like an electric fence, hoping to shock his ego.

We're two worshipers trying to prove our superior intimacy with and appreciation of a goddess—Christopher using his experience as her classmate, me using my physical proximity as her boyfriend. This lasts for an hour, and a bottle of Chardonnay.

Then the buzzer rings, and in the time it takes Jane to climb the stairs, Christopher skims a few lines from the stack of poems I've placed in my lap. "Not bad," he says in an offhand way, which even I—buzzing with desperation and alcohol—know he doesn't mean.

Jane walks in and shakes the snow off her hair. She looks at Christopher. "Why are you wearing underwear?" she asks, her guilelessness as cold and crisp as her lips when we kiss hello.

"Partywear," says Christopher, taking Jane's coat.

Then he lights the candles on the dinner table, adding a few more flickers to the dozens surrounding us, and we all sit down to eat.

Jane is a scholarship student supporting herself with grants and loans and part-time jobs, one as a mother's helper for a jet-setting socialite.

"She makes me wear a surgical mask around her boy," says Jane. "She's insane."

"I think masks are sexy," says Christopher, candlelight flickering off his chest hairs.

"Sickness builds your immune system," says Jane, ignoring Christopher, sounding like her German mother, a university professor who, I suspect, owns a first edition of Darwin. "She'd rather snort coke with Mick Jagger than deal with her child."

"Mick *Jagger*?" Christopher and I say in unison, instantly forged into a single star-worshiping organism. "Have you met him?"

"I've seen him in her living room," says Jane. "He treats me like a servant."

And why wouldn't he?

"I'm going to write her a letter," says Jane. "I'm going to tell her she's destroying her child."

"She'll fire you," we say, Christopher and I agreeing that a job with access to the preeminent rock star of our time is worth overlooking the foibles of an unfit, drug-addled mother.

"I don't care," says Jane. "It's the right thing to do."

As is usually the case when seminarians have supper, sooner or later the table talk turns to the Old and the New Testaments. I've never read either, my scholarly expertise being the old and the new Bugs Bunny (drawn by the Moses and Paul of animators, Tex Avery and Chuck Jones, respectively). So I keep my mouth full of the chicken in mustard sauce that Christopher calls "*supreme* in Dijonaise," nodding periodically in this "I totally understand what you mean, but I'm too busy eating *supreme* in Dijonaise to talk" way. Then, thank God, the meal is over, and Jane and I walk to the love seat, where Christopher brings us slices of pumpkin pie with whipped cream. This, I understand. Pie makes me feel at home. I'm enjoying myself again.

Christopher walks over to the mahogany armoire set against one wall, opens it, and turns on the radio. "Happy Birthday to the Chairman of the Board," says the dj. "All Sinatra, all night." Frank sings "Start spreading the news . . ."

Christopher takes Jane's plate from her lap, sets it down on the coffee table, and dances her around the room, like Fred and Ginger, only if Fred were openly bisexual, barefoot, and more boudoir than debonair.

I watch. Because that's what I do when people dance. Actual dancing requires knowledge and skill, finesse. Confidence—being able to lead a woman where you want her to go, slowly. Deferred gratification. Manly qualities. Qualities I don't possess. Versus the bestial, instinctive grinding of a predator against his prey: hind-legged, clothes-on copulating in 4/4 time. *That* I can do.

Which is why I am upset. Once again, Christopher has shown himself the better man: the better cook, better student, better poet, and, now, the better dancer, a lesson I already learned at the gay and lesbian dance, his tongue flickering to the beat as he moved toward Jane under the disco ball. Fucker!

But a mouth full of pie is enough to push jealousy back down into the bile from whence it came, so I keep eating.

Christopher won't let me be. He dips Jane backward, right beside me. Even if my father weren't a bomber pilot and I didn't have excellent peripheral vision, it would be impossible not to see them out of the corner of my eye, Christopher with his big bisexual pie-eating grin, Jane clearly enjoying herself, more horizontal than vertical—more *Kama Sutra* than *The Gay Divorcee*.

Keep your eye on the pie, James, eye on the pie. I look straight ahead and down at the plate, constricting my field of vision from panoramic to a small slice of the ocular pie, maybe one or two degrees, like a warm-blooded ninja ostrich. I don't need sand to hide *my* head! After one more nutmeggy bite, I've forgotten everything.

Then two fingers enter the closed airspace directly over my lap, a no-fly zone if ever there was one; index and middle, poised, like a double-barreled dragonfly, or the number 11—with joints and little brown knuckle hairs. There's no way not to see them, except to close my eyes or look away. But closing my eyes or looking away from two hairy fingers hovering over my zipper— and my pie—well, that is a bridge of denial too far, even for me. But, as light travels faster than the ability to process the visual information, I just watch as the fingers dip down and scrape the whipped cream off my slice, like a hawk plucking a winter hare from his pumpkin patch, then taking off again, leaving only white streaks where a moment ago there'd been a dollop of cream I'd been carefully apportioning to accompany each bite of pie. It's hard to know which is more upsetting—that my body is being violated or that my perfect cream/pie ratio is being thwarted. Do I value personal space? Or order?

Before I can answer my question, Christopher's goggle-eyed face appears alongside mine, millimeters away, accompanied by his now cream-coated fingers. He daubs my cheek. *Ugh.* (There goes personal space and order.) Then as the Chairman of the Board hits his final chorus and the horns hit their final notes, Christopher opens his mouth, unfurls his long, wet, bristly, feral tongue, just as he did at the gay and lesbian dance, only instead of kissing Jane, he licks the cream clean off my face like a cat grooming his privates.

There are some feelings that even a bite of pie can't tamp down. One of them is a man licking my face. I look up at Jane to see how she plans to handle this. Yes, it's my body. But it's her friend. And she's the graduate student; she's more mature. *And* she's a woman. She's got a lot more experience fending off advances from deviant sexual predators. I've never had to say no to anybody, except myself when self-love started coming between getting out of bed in the morning and going to class on time. Most of all, Jane doesn't care what people think of her. She can send back my dish at a restaurant over my mortified objections, allowing me to berate her for being pushy while eating the delicious replacement dish her pushy personality made possible *and* then still being friends with the waiter—good cop/bad cop. Just as I can be friends with Christopher after she tells him, as of course she will, to back off.

But Jane's not saying anything. She's just standing there in the arms of a man who's wearing silk underwear and who has just licked my cheek; two future masters of divinity, both seeming to tell me, You're a big girl now.

Theoretically, I'm as into perverted sex as the next guy, but not *with* the next guy. I look up at Christopher and say, "I'm not really into guys licking whipped cream off my cheek," a straightforward message delivered in a straightforward, even friendly way; a neutral statement of fact—perhaps at variance with the subtext of my message: Get the fuck away from me, you deviant motherfucker; that was the most disgusting thing a man has ever done to me. But, unlike Jane, I hate open conflict. And I still want Christopher to read my poems. I want him to think I have talent. Yes, he's as profoundly unattractive as he is aggressive, which is *very*, not to mention male, which, when the subject of potential sexual couplings comes up, knocks me out of the discussion. But he's also *really* fucking smart. And such is the double helix of artistic DNA sometimes. Frank Sinatra was definitely friends with gangsters and possibly a gangster himself, and listening to him now, I realize if there's a more honest singing voice, I haven't heard it.

Christopher says, "If you cut your hair any shorter, you could be a member of the Résistance." He says it with a French accent—like that's supposed to mean something, other than I'm resistant. Which I am. For the first time, I see the ropes and pulleys of his mind: He took the fact that I'm resisting him, called it "Résistance" with a French accent, then built a quip around it that included my hair. It's really quite mechanical, and, for a moment, sad. Perhaps this is what Cassius Clay felt in the ring when he saw Sonny Liston's guard go down: This man is beatable.

Without missing a beat, Christopher turns off the radio and walks to a closed door. "Want to see the rest of the apartment?"

Jane lives in a little dorm room in one of the seminary buildings. I live in 150 roach- and vermin-infested square feet in Harlem, where the roaches are as long as cigarillos and the mattress is convex, forcing Jane and me to sleep on opposite edges of the V, where the springs still work, balanced on our hip bones. Anyplace with an interior door is a mansion, and mansions are for exploring.

Christopher opens the door and flicks on a dimmer. The three of us walk into a bedroom.

I see the three of us looking back from the walls and the ceiling. Almost everything is covered in mirrors. Everything that isn't mirrored is lacquered in shiny red and black—even the headboard of the water bed, which gurgles in waves when Christopher plops down on the black bedspread to demonstrate.

On one lacquered chest, there's an old 8mm gunmetal gray reel-to-reel projector.

Christopher stands up and switches it on, filling the little screen and all the mirrors around and above us with a jerky black-and-white film.

Whether it's the shock or the Chardonnay, it takes a moment to understand what we're looking at: a hugely endowed man pummeling a woman from behind while she kneels on a bed, fellating another hugely endowed man who is standing in front of her—two men, one woman, in a bedroom. Just like the three of us.

Christopher waggles one of his whipped creamers at the man being fellated and says, "That's Rod Cummings." It's a name I've read more than once in lurid letters on the marquees of X-rated movie theaters on Forty-second Street. "This is his apartment," says Christopher. "He's my friend." Like being friends with a porn star is a badge of honor.

Jane, who knows more about divinity than pornography, points to the man in the rear. "Who is *that*?"

"John Holmes," says Christopher.

"Who's John Holmes?"

"Ask James," says Christopher, like I know as much about porn as he does.

"Do you know who he is?" asks Jane.

"A porn star," I say, because I do know as much about porn as

Christopher does, maybe even more. Finally a human endeavor in which Christopher and I are peers!

I've never watched a pornographic film with Jane. She's not that kind of woman. So watching Rod Cummings and John Holmes and the kneeling woman together is both exciting and darkly exciting payback to Jane for watching Christopher lick me. For a moment, Christopher and I are on the same side: defiling Jane together, although Christopher, bless the homosexual chamber of his bisexual heart, probably thinks he's turning her on.

Jane says, "Is that what I think it is?" She's giving Christopher the benefit of the doubt—like there's a story line; as though these people are going to put their clothes back on and do something besides take them off again; like we're looking at silent, pixilated, black-and-white Charlie Chaplin. Jane's guilelessness is sometimes hard to believe.

Christopher says, "What do you think it is?" answering Jane's question with a question. (Note to undergraduate self: Remember this technique when you graduate.)

Jane, realizing that this *is* what she thinks it is, says, "Why would I want to watch *that*? Turn it off."

Christopher does.

A few moments later, Jane and I are sitting on a red-and-black lacquered chest, our eyes closed, kissing.

Christopher sits down next to us and places his palms on our backs, like the minister he's training to become, to partake of our bond, to remind us he's here, as though maybe we've forgotten to include him in the pas de deux, which should really be a ménage à trois. Only instead of expanding the circuit and adding energy to our coupling, he's trying to take it away, like a pump, or a vampire.

I scrunch my eyes, like Dorothy in *The Wizard of Oz,* hoping Jane's kiss will transport us back home, to the seminary. When I open my eyes, Christopher is looking right at us through strangely dilated pupils, like a hungry, emaciated, cross-dressing wolf. Perhaps it's just the thick, owlish glasses. Either way, I can see he needs even more attention than I do, and that the depth of his need is bottomless. It's terrifying.

Jane says, "I think we should go."

A few minutes later, Jane and I are in our coats, descending the old wooden staircase, Christopher looking down from the top of the landing, his arms and legs wrapped around the post of the banister, like a crumpled, barefoot satyr in silken Jesus party-wear trying to hug or hump himself. "Don't go," he says.

Jane keeps walking.

I turn and say, "We have to," slowing my step, talking up at Christopher over my shoulder, trying to end the evening on a friendly note. Jane has the confidence to tell a waiter her boyfriend doesn't like the food. But salving the hurt feelings of a waiter, or a spurned bisexual predator—that's my strength. "I'm sorry."

Christopher says, "It's not fair."

And he's right. I get to go home with a lovely, cultivated woman. While brilliant, cultivated Christopher spends the night alone on Rod Cummings's water bed, staring up at himself in a mirrored ceiling, wearing a cream-colored kimono and matching silk diaper, in the flickering light of an 8mm silent porno film.

"It's not fair," says Christopher again, to himself, it seems to me, and to God—he *is* an Old Testament scholar—as much as to the two of us, or to me anyway. Jane, one can see, feels no obligation whatsoever to explain why she's leaving in haste, why she's not willing to be the cream filling in the vanilla sandwich Christopher is proposing.

I reach the landing and take a long look back at mahogany and silk. What a nice banister. What a sad man wrapping himself around it. I want to pacify Christopher, make things right again, return us all to where we were a few hours ago, when the only ulterior motives that mattered were mine.

I turn and step through the front door and into the snow, holding my still-unblessed-by-Christopher poems in one hand and, in the other, their muse, Jane, who walks down the sidewalk with no need to discuss that what Christopher just did was wrong and what she did was right.

No wonder she thinks that Jesus loves her, and, to be fair, everyone. Not that I've read the New Testament, or the Old, but from what I've heard—from Jane, and Christopher—God has always favored those who see the world in black and white.

I, on the other hand, see shades of gray, mixed blessings, wherever I go. And I could do Christopher the favor of telling him the dark side of female charisma: that someone who often thinks she's right rarely thinks she's wrong. I could comfort Christopher with that knowledge. I could ease his pain right now. *I* could be the Christian among us.

I could do all of this, had that twisted motherfucker actually read my poems.

EIGHT

Plus 1

Another day in just an ordinary life
Ordinary problems: mother, father, husband, wife
I'm looking for a way to cut my ordinary ties
I'll find something, or die
—song, year two

Inviting my girlfriend Jane to San Antonio to meet my sister Corinne, the only member of my family Jane had never met, on the weekend Corinne was to be married really did seem like a good idea. I was proud of my girlfriend, just as Corinne was proud of her fiancé, whom I had never met. This way, we'd get to meet each other's sweethearts and deepen the familial connection all the way around. That was the thinking.

But when Jane and I got back to the hotel after a walk along the river, ready to get dressed for Corinne's wedding rehearsal, I started having second thoughts, and then third and fourth thoughts, as I was reminded what a familial connection actually means in my family. When the elevator door opened to our floor, I could hear a woman weeping. As I got farther down the hall, closer to my room, I could tell the weeping was in my mom's room, right next to mine, and that I was related to the weeper: my sister Kate. Kate is given to drama, melodrama even, but these did not sound like crocodile tears. So I pressed my ear to the door to find out what was going on. Jane, at my direction, pressed her opposite ear, the peephole between us, in case someone looked out. Jane was facing me in confusion. A direct and guileless person, she evidently had never engaged in pre–family reunion ear-to-the-hotel-room-door incognito surveillance. (We were still getting to know each other, Jane and I, even after a few years.) Hopefully, hotel security was on another floor.

Jane said, "Why don't you go in?"

I said, "Shhh!" Then I whispered, "I need to know what happened first." To prepare. I was an English major; I believed that all the world's a stage. In my family tragedy, it helped to know the other characters' lines.

But all I could tell was that my entire family was in there, except for Corinne. And they were debating whether to leave San Antonio *before* the wedding—where we had all flown to attend.

I looked at Jane to help me make sense of this news. She looked at me as if to say, Knock on the door and find out what the hell is going on.

So I knocked on the door.

My stepdad, Norman, opened up.

Looking inside, I saw what reminded me of the dayroom in a psychiatric inpatient unit. (In my family, there are two kinds of people: patients and visitors.) All the faces suggested both visibly extreme and dissociated emotional states; everyone avoided everyone else's gaze; only, unlike those in the psych ward, these patients were attired in suits and cocktail dresses, the furniture was upholstered in damask brocade, and the medicine was served in cocktail glasses instead of in paper pill cups. In one corner, Kate sat on a desk chair, heaving, convulsing really, like an epileptic in fancy makeup, mascara running down her cheeks, which made her look like a raccoon in the rain. A trash can sat nearby, just in case, I later learned, she vomited again before she could get to the bathroom. My mom was sitting on the lounge chair, Ferragamo-pumped feet up on the ottoman, ashen-skinned, hollow-eyed, a wadded tissue in one of her hands. She was looking at the padded arm, like it might spontaneously burst into flame and tell her how to lead her people from this emotional desert. My stepdad was standing, arms crossed, staring out the window at downtown San Antonio, perhaps wondering whether his first marriage, to the occasional blackout drunk who supposedly tried to burn down his house, might, all things considered, have been the better marriage. My brother was sitting on the foot of the bed, leaning over, his arms were resting on his thighs, hands clenched, like there was no use in fighting anymore. He was looking into the middle distance at a painting of the Alamo—a visual reminder that sometimes good people get their scalps chopped clean off, right here in downtown San Antonio.

I closed the door behind me. "What happened?" I asked.

Kate started sobbing, my question evidently triggering a painful memory.

"We were just trying to help . . ." said my mom, trailing off into post-traumatic stress disorder silence.

As at any crime scene, you have to engage in a bit of Detective Columboesque forensic reconstruction to piece together the sequence of events. After interviewing everyone, as near as I could tell, this is what happened: Corinne asked Kate, who was a professional singer, to perform the wedding song as Corinne walked down the aisle tomorrow. Kate decided she needed to rehearse the song tonight, at the wedding rehearsal, her thinking being that this was what wedding rehearsals were for, in addition to the fact she suffered from stage fright—and sister fright. She was terrified of screwing up on the biggest day of her big sister's life. But the piano player Corinne had hired *a year ago* was not available to rehearse tonight, because he was the most famous (and therefore busy) piano player in San Antonio; that's why Corinne had hired him a year ago. He showed up one time only: at your wedding, where he played from sheet music, perfectly, with or without a singer. So, faced with the singer barfing in anticipatory stage and sister fright, and a piano player who could not ameliorate the terror by rehearsing, my mom fired the piano player today, the day before the wedding, without first asking the bride; she didn't want to bother the bride with more details, she said. As the replacement pianist, my mom hired the first musician she could find: the music student playing "Greensleeves" in the hotel lobby; he was available to rehearse. "We all thought he sounded lovely," said my mom. "Didn't we, Earl?" She was trying to get the buy-in from my brother. "He's a very nice young man," said my mom. Hiring him meant Kate would be calm and Corinne would be happy.

When Corinne found out that my mom had fired the piano player she had hired *a year ago,* on the day before her wedding, she was not happy. As they say in the dayroom of a psychiatric inpatient unit, she went nuts.

Hence, the debate: to attend or not to attend Corinne's wedding.

"It's too embarrassing to cancel," said my mom finally. "All my friends are here." Saving face was obviously a higher family value than risking additional psychotic outbursts. "We'll arrive as a family," said my mom, like a matriarch whose throne is a lounge chair, her scepter a glass of white wine, her orb a ball of wadded tissues. "We'll be polite and respectful. Then we'll leave as a family, after the ceremony."

Jane and I are walking arm in arm in a two-by-two wedding-rehearsal procession down a lighted flagstone path that leads to the back garden of the Argyle Club, a former plantation house in San Antonio.

Thirty years ago, my mom made her debut into San Antonio society here, escorted by General Eisenhower's personal pilot— the man who would become my father. He was between wars at the time, having firebombed the Germans but not the North Koreans, and in the meantime, he was flying Ike around the country by day and escorting debs to fancy dress balls by night— the last debutante being my mom, creating a partnership that, according to my dad, was far more traumatic than being shot down at night in a B-26 over Pyongyang. And my dad actually *was* shot down at night in a B-26 over Pyongyang. When your bomber's going down in flames, you can theoretically parachute to safety, an impossible task when confronted with battalions of divorce lawyers with affidavits, family-court judges with restraining orders, and forensic psychiatrists with admitting privileges to psychiatric hospitals. Being a war hero is a lot easier than being a husband, or a father, at least when you're my dad.

So when his firstborn, my sister Corinne, gets married tomorrow, right here, where it all began, he'll be a thousand miles away, in Tulsa, with his third wife; he knows how this story ends. Why read it again?

My mom, who has a library of Book-of-the-Month Club romance novels about the predictable and yet tragically alluring pitfalls of marriage and remarriage, is here with her fourth and—she says—favorite husband, Norman, standing at the front of the procession, followed by Kate and Earl, and then Jane and me—all of us dressed for the occasion.

As is the Argyle Club: The manicured grass is divided into left and right columns of white folding chairs, one side for guests of the bride, the other for guests of the groom. The two sides are separated by an aisle with a white satin runner leading to a satin-covered platform where the vows will be exchanged— all framed by wrought-iron torch lamps, dotted by flowering magnolia trees, and edged in flower beds.

At one end of the garden is a grand staircase leading up to the house, its covered back porch busy with waiters quietly setting formal tables. The only sounds are the snap of starched white linen tablecloths and the occasional ping of crystal or clank of silver and china. It's the apogee of soothing, understated antebellum elegance.

Then Corinne appears at the top of the staircase and, seeing my mom, and evidently still upset with her for firing the piano player (sometimes one outburst does not have a palliative, mollifying effect on anger), she literally runs down the steps, her heels clicking with the *rat-tat-tat* of a Gatling gun—a sound whose urgency matches the fury on Corinne's face. Her expression, like everyone else's in my mom's hotel room today, would be more at home in a psychiatric inpatient unit than at a wedding rehearsal—only instead of someone in the dayroom, Corinne looks more like someone locked in the quiet room, where the door is locked from the outside. Dressed in an emerald green satin dress that billows in the breeze of her rapid descent, a copy of *Wedding Etiquette* by Emily Post opened and spread on her bodice under one manicured hand, the other hand scratching the air with the talons of a bird of prey coming in for a landing, Corinne glances around, her radiant raven tresses framing what are either wild or as-yet-undiagnosed (and therefore unmedicated) hyperthyroid eyes. She looks like the belle of a burning ball, like Vivien Leigh running away from Tara—with the bug eyes of Peter Lorre and the piercing shriek of a pterodactyl in a sci-fi thriller. She's an A-movie *and* a B-movie star, a statuesque glamour girl and a flying dinosaur, all rolled into five feet, eleven inches of volcanic rage. When she hits the landing, Corinne digs her nails into my mom's arm and screams, "You think you can destroy me! I will destroy *you!*" Heels clicking on the slate, teeth literally bared, Corinne drags my mom off the path, onto the lawn, and under a magnolia tree to feast on her prey.

In some families, a scene like this—a mother being attacked by one of her children—might inspire the mother's other children (me, my brother, and my sister Kate), or, for that matter, the mother's consort (my stepfather, Norman), to rush to the mother's defense in a kind of immediate, instinctive, involuntary response many people call "love." But as Tolstoy might have written had he read a little more Freud, every grossly dysfunctional family is grossly dysfunctional in its own way. In this family, the love toward a mother or a wife is trumped by the love of self, specifically a love of one's own ass, which needs to be protected against the onslaught of a sister or a stepdaughter who is in the midst of a psychotic breakdown. There is no way anyone is going anywhere near *that*. Everyone is looking away from the others, perhaps hoping they will make it go away, and, in the meantime, finding their own little private corner of the dayroom of the mind. My stepdad, the theoretical man of the family, is looking at my mom through the beady, "Detach with Love" eyes he cultivated at the Al-Anon meetings during his first marriage and seeing not *his* wife, but *our* mother. She's *our* responsibility. My sister Kate, heaving with terrifying flashbacks (to this afternoon), is looking at *our* mother and seeing our stepdad's wife. She's *his* responsibility. My brother, Earl, is looking down at his handmade shoes, not seeing anything but the reflection of the sunset. Even the waiters are looking away, champagne flutes and sterling knives frozen in their hands, the clinking and clanking of place settings brought to a silent standstill. The only sound is Corinne's screaming. My mom is on her own.

"I know you're a little nervous about getting married tomorrow, honey," says my mom, with a level of understatement that makes the Argyle Club seem flamboyant. The rest of us look on in a pained but hopeful way, as though rooting for the mouse to escape from the cat.

"Don't give me that crap, Mother!" says Corinne. "Mother," instead of "Mom," being a peculiar linguistic choice that divides me from my siblings. "You're jealous of me! And you know it!"

"That's not true," says my mom, her head hanging down like the coquettish debutante she was thirty years ago. Only now she's trying to attract sympathy instead of a husband. "I want you to be happy."

"Bullshit!" shrieks Corinne.

It hurts to see people you love hurt each other, but who am I to tamper with human nature? I observe, just like everyone else in my family, all of us having retreated to the safety of individual magnolia trees. Unlike Tolstoy, we've been to psychotherapy and recognize this as a boundary issue.

Except for Jane, whose father's drug of choice was whiskey, not psychotherapy, and therefore she was never psychoanalyzed into believing that the world is a restaurant and that, for the most part, when someone asks you for a glass of water, you say, "This is not my table." Instead, Jane says, "Do something!" as though a bride attacking her mother is not normal, not grasping the fact that my coming between the bride and her mother is equally not normal, and terrifying. As is the prospect of losing Jane. I can see in her frightened eyes that my stock as a man is declining by the decibel. It's one thing to lose her because my family is nuts. That can't be helped. And her family is just as problematic, so we're peers in the relative insanity department. But she is not afraid to speak truth to powerful insanity, and I *am* afraid. And if I can't get over this fear, right now, Jane and

I are doomed. And losing her and being alone with *them,* my flesh and blood . . . well, that's even scarier than defending my flesh and blood from my flesh and blood.

I walk over to the magnolia tree and say to Corinne, "Don't talk to your mother like that!" in the hope that Corinne will bow to the universally recognized second-person value that attacking *your* mother isn't cool, versus the morally relative first- or third-person value that attacking *my* mother or *our* mother can be justified in certain circumstances, like these.

It works! Corinne releases my mom's arm, yielding to the universally recognized second-person value: shame. If I'd known how easy it was to be assertive, I would have introduced civility into this family a long time ago!

Then Corinne turns her dilated pupils on me and screams, "Stay out!"

I start trembling, like Kate. I knew this was a mistake. I'm not qualified to confront a visibly and audibly unhinged older sibling on the eve of the most important day of her life.

Jane walks up behind me. "He's just trying to help," she offers.

Corinne screams, "Stay out! You weren't even invited!" alluding to the fact that Jane is a "Plus 1" on the guest list, not a guest in her own right.

Jane bursts into tears, joining my mom and Kate in the chorus of weeping women in cocktail dresses and fancy jewelry who are trembling under magnolia trees.

The men continue staring into the middle distance or down at their just-shined shoes. As does the entire staff of the Argyle Club, all of whom are unwilling or unable to intervene, as though they are enchanted.

And then there's me, bubbling now with a homicidal rage I haven't felt since I was eighteen years old, managing my brother's restaurant, and a drifter pulled a knife on me and demanded the cash in the drawer. I saw a hammer popping out from the blind side of the counter, where the drifter couldn't see it, and I thought to grab it and pound the drifter's head like a nail. But I didn't want to live on as a murdering carpenter. And I didn't want to die if I missed his head and he killed me. So I left the hammer alone, gave the drifter all the money, and watched him walk away.

Corinne is robbing me, too, but of dignity, if I even have any left. It's one thing for my sister to insult my mother. This really is *their* relationship. And my mom should not have fired the piano player without asking the bride. But for my sister to insult my girlfriend—even though my girlfriend should have kept her mouth shut and not tried to fill the vacuum of leadership—*that* feels like an attack on *me*. And as we've all learned, no one in this family defends you against an attack when the person attacking you is another member of the family. You're on your own.

I say, "How dare you!"

Corinne parries this challenge by suddenly gripping my throat with one hand, her other still holding *Wedding Etiquette*. Evidently, she's heard enough out of my insolent mouth, whose air supply she is now constricting, while still managing her responsibilities as a wedding planner. A lot of women can multitask, I'll grant you that. But how many can emotionally destabilize and intimidate an entire family, violently suppress an insurrection, *and* plan a wedding—all at the same time? She is amazing.

Nevertheless, this is no time for idle or idol worship. I can't breathe. So like any little brother being semistrangled by his big sister, I grip my neck reflexively to peel off her fingers. But Corinne sewed as a child, and I think she owns Jack LaLanne handgrips. *Plus,* she's five eleven—all of it pumped with the adrenaline that flows from attacking one's mother in public, and then one's brother. Her fingers are locked in place like the jaw of a rottweiler.

Following her example, and going one hand better, I take my hands off my neck, wrap them around hers, and squeeze.

At which point, like anyone being strangled—even the world's most angry multitasking wedding planner—Corinne drops *Wedding Etiquette* on the manicured grass, freeing up her other manicured hand, and allowing her to sink her other five shiny nails into my throat.

So now we're both strangling each other with both hands with no exit strategy other then loss of consciousness.

Then someone with a drawl from West Texas, or maybe from too many beers, or both, says, "What seems to be the problem?"

I turn, mid-strangle, and meet Jack, Corinne's fiancé: thirty something, red nose on a sallow face framed in big square glasses, like a hunk of nearsighted wine and cheddar cheese stuck on top of a tuxedo. "Howdy, brother."

I let go of Corinne. Corinne lets go of me.

I shake Jack's hand. "Pleased to meet you."

Corinne collapses on Jack's shoulder, shaking and sobbing like all the other women now, mascara smudging her cheeks— like a Miami Dolphin sweating on game day, only in a shimmering green satin dress instead of an iridescent uniform.

Jane walks over to me and weeps into my arms.

"How could she marry . . . *him*?" I say, reflected, projected vanity being a higher family value than outrage, injustice, and/or morality. Violent memories fade with time. But a hideous brother-in-law and his offspring are forever.

The other couples emerge from the magnolia trees and reunite: my mom and Norman; Kate and Earl.

The waiters murmur back to life.

My throat stings. I rub it, then look at my fingertips.

"You're bleeding!" says Jane, as though I were blind.

That night at the Argyle Club, the wedding party is sitting at a big horseshoe-shaped table in a private room.

Jack's best man, Timmy, is standing up on a little stage in front, where the horseshoe opens, toasting the groom. "We sure are gonna miss you on those cruises down the Rio Grande," says Timmy to Jack. "We had some good times, buddy. The beer, the hookers. Maria says 'Hi, and adios, hombre!' "

Jack laughs along with the rest of his friends.

Corinne looks like she did when she dug her nails into my mom's arm, and into my throat.

I laugh at Timmy as I would laugh at a cartoon character who's blithely unaware that an anvil is dropping from the sky, about to flatten him. I get up from my chair on one side of the horseshoe and walk over to the other side to check on my mom, trying to slink unnoticed past Corinne.

She's at the top of the horseshoe, her back turned. But like most superior predators, she possesses superior peripheral vision; she reels me in by my lapel. "He has no idea that by this time tomorrow he'll be driving back to West Texas without having been at his best friend's wedding," says Corinne, sounding like Peter Lorre with a bubbly laugh. Then, in a soft, kittenish voice, she asks, "Are you having a good time?" as if reciting from a page out of *Wedding Etiquette*.

I say, "Um, yeah," feeling wary and whiplashed between Corinne's twin poles.

"Sorry if I got a little upset," she says.

"That's okay," I say. The dried blood on my neck is just more water under the bridge. We know how to make up.

Jane walks over.

Corinne takes Jane by the hand and pulls her close and thanks her for coming, as though she's a bona fide guest, not a Plus 1.

Jane looks at me as if to say, I don't understand.

I give Jane a look that says, Not now!

We stand there as the toasts continue, Jane and I, Corinne seated between us, her hands wrapped around us, sharing a warm, familial embrace, looking out at my mom and my third stepdad, Kate and Earl, Jack and his doomed best man, eating and drinking and laughing, like it's any other day.

NINE

February 14

She don't know what she don't know most of the time
No, she don't know what she don't know
And that's fine
—song

At *my* wedding, Kate did the flowers. So I know she is both discerning and extravagant—plus, she has a preternatural ability to sense what you've spent, and *why* you spent it. (Because it was the right choice? Or because it was on sale?) And she *is* terminally ill. So as I'm standing in the middle of an open-air flower shack in Houston, alongside Corinne, who just picked me up from the airport, looking in a refrigerator case at roses for Kate, there's a lot riding on the decision. I won't get a second chance to make a first impression. This is the last bouquet.

Or maybe not. The flower shack is run by Israelis and Mexicans, an ethnic partnership I've never seen, not even in New York. Maybe anything really is possible. Maybe Kate is going to live.

After some discussion with Schlomo, the salesman, and a tour of the refrigerated dark red coffin toppers, I propose yellow long stems. We *are* in Texas, Kate's alive, and hope springs eternal. Corinne agrees, as long as we put the long stems in a globe-shaped vase. I hate globe-shaped vases—they are squat and ugly—and I don't want one being Kate's final impression of how I feel for her—or her last evidence of my bad taste.

But like the Israelis and the Mexicans, Corinne and I have an unlikely partnership, too. A globe-shaped vase it is. Schlomo says in that case, we'll need two dozen long stems to fill the huge hole, and he suggests mixing in extra rose petals with the water, so the stems won't look so lonely in there, floating around in all that empty space. "For you," he says, "fifty dollars. No tax." We wait a few minutes, until Pedro, the florist, comes over. He cuts our long stems down to about six inches, the size of cheap roses, so they'll fit inside the globe.

The globe is on my lap and my lap is in Corinne's car and Corinne's car is on the stretch of road leading from the flower shacks—an actual district of them, like the bordellos that pop up around an army base, only here the bloom is still on the rose. We're heading to the city of hope: the Medical Center, multiple hospitals that—according to the signs on the road—treat women and children; for this disease, that condition. Tower after tower after tower, visible from miles around on the flat horizon, rising like a medical Oz: a place where miracles are actually performed on a daily basis. I'd like to bring my marriage here.

When we get to Methodist Hospital, we pull in to the parking garage and look for a spot—on the first level, then the second level, then the third. Nothing but cars. Around and around we go—up, up, up the concrete spiral, until we get to the roof, to the sun, and emptiness. Not a car in sight. I wonder why.

Then I open my door, and remember: I am on a roof in Houston, and a roof in Houston is for scorpions and salamanders and other cold-blooded creatures who live in the desert. It's 100 degrees in the winter! And I *like* it! It's alive. Sunny. It makes me think of Kate—of how she'd like it up here, of how the least preferred of all places sometimes is the best.

The yellow roses do not like it here, however. So we take the elevator to the tenth floor, check in with the nursing station, and walk down a linoleum-tiled hall.

There—visible through the window between a hospital room and the ICU—which they now call the CCU (critical is the new intensive)—lies my sister Kate. Her face is covered in tubes that feed air into a mask. Other tubes and wires connect her to a glucose IV drip and a morphine drip, a machine monitoring her blood pressure, another for her heart rate, a third for her oxygen saturation. The IV is inserted into her jugular vein, which is surrounded by a network of little portals, all of which are taped shut. Her eyes are shut. Her head is bald.

I'm terrified.

I walk in to her room.

She opens her eyes and says, "Hunt!" and leans up from her bed.

I lean down.

We embrace, and both of us burst into tears. It's the saddest I have ever felt.

We hold each other for several minutes, Corinne looking on from the foot of the bed. It feels awkward—crying in "public," telling Kate that I love her. Notwithstanding that Corinne is my family.

Kate says, "I'm dying, Hunt." Without any reservations. Diva-like. Whatever stage fright she may have had when singing at Corinne's wedding twenty years ago has evaporated in the confidence-boosting heat of terminal cancer.

We cry some more, in waves.

Then there's a long-enough lull for me to give Kate the roses.

"They're so beautiful," Kate says, in her barely breathing, drug-addled way. I can see it in her face: She really likes them. Especially the globe. Corinne understands Kate in a way I never will.

I set the globe on the rolling tray table, next to the box of tissues and the lotion.

Becky, the nurse, walks in and says, "Those are beautiful! Do you know what day it is, Kate?"

Kate says, "The day I'm going to die?" And she laughs.

We all laugh, like it's a joke.

Becky says, "No, silly. It's Valentine's Day." Obviously, she doesn't know—and how could she?—that in my family, holidays are generally not causes for celebration, for the simple reason that holidays are the only times of the year when we see one another. And when we see one another, we usually remind one another of why we haven't seen one another since the last holiday.

TEN

Cancer for Christmas

Flew in to my hometown this afternoon
My lover right beside me
I knew when we touched down
She'd feel it, too
That something that divides me
—song, year three

It's Christmas morning in Denver, my hometown, and I'm sitting on the living room floor by the tree with Jane, whom I've brought from New York to take the mom test.

Which won't be easy. Not that my mom doesn't like Jane; she does, more than any other girlfriend I've brought home. But she's not crazy about me, because I remind her of my dad, whom I remind of my mom. So being associated with me is not necessarily an advantage when trying impress either of my parents, but especially my mom, whom everyone in my family and three stepfamilies has failed to impress at one time or another. Starting with my father, who failed the mom test and lost the custody battle, his one remaining fatherly function being to warn me about "your mother" and "her children," who are also his children. One of them being Kate, the most recent among us to be cast out of the family, this time for finally finding a husband: a cocaine trafficker who, to his credit, paid his debt to society—in San Quentin. Leaving as the current Christmas lineup Corinne and Earl, who are back in the fold, for the moment; me, of course, for one week a year; my third stepdad, Norman, who, my mom did recently reassure, is her favorite husband . . . so far; and at the center of it all, my mother, curled up on the living room sofa in her nightgown, moaning with a blocked colon. The doctor who x-rayed her last night in the ER after she keeled over at dinner recommended unblocking it then, but she postponed the surgery until tomorrow so she could see the joy on our faces today as we open her presents.

I open mine: a huge beige London Fog trench coat like Detective Colombo wears, only in XXL. Sale size.

I say, "Thanks, Mom."

My mom says, "It rains a lot in New York, honey. Ugggh." Talking squeezes her colon.

I say, "It does rain in New York."

"Try it on," says my mom. "Uggh. Oh, you look so handsome! Ugghhh." Her taste in clothes is clearly perverted by the pain. I could not look less debonair, or more clownlike. If the coat had a line of buttons sewn up the spine, I could close it in the back.

Then it's Jane's turn: a key lime sweater, as too small as my coat is too large; too tight to fit a twelve-year-old girl before puberty, and Jane is a robust, Germanic twenty-six; her cup, a 34B.

Having grown up in a family where telling the truth is a virtue, Jane whispers, "What do I say?"

I whisper, "Tell her you like it."

"*I don't.*"

"*Just tell her!*"

Jane says, "It's so . . . *colorful.* Thank you!"

That night, in a private mother-son moment, my mom says, "I think Jane would make you a good wife."

The next day, we all drive my mom to the hospital for the operation. It's supposed to be routine, and I'm still limping around in my knee brace from major knee surgery a month ago, so operations don't really scare me. So after my mom goes into the operating room and we wait an appropriate amount of time to seem concerned, my brother tells my sister Corinne that we're going for a walk.

Then as we'd planned, he and Jane and I walk or hobble on crutches to the car and drive to TJ Maxx to exchange our Christmas presents for cash, like we do every year the day after Christmas. My mom's presents this year (my brother got the same trench coat, which, as he is skinnier than I am, looked even worse on him than it did on me) are more ill-fitting and generally ill-advised than normal. She hasn't really understood our taste since the board games, or maybe sporting-goods phase, a long time ago now. Though in her defense, we don't spend much time together anymore. But we still like money, and we figure as our mother, she wants to make us happy. So . . .

Jane's a little uncomfortable with the idea, even though she hates the sweater as much as we hate our trench coats. "What if your mom finds out?" she says as we're standing in line at the TJ Maxx customer service desk.

My brother says, "Not possible."

I say, "Relax, Jane. This is a family tradition."

Jane hands her sweater to the clerk and takes the cash, like a member of the family.

And we all drive back to the hospital to be with my mom when she wakes up, unblocked.

As we step through the automatic doors, Corinne rushes down the hall at us, heels clicking on the linoleum, mascara running down her cheeks, her still as-yet-undiagnosed and therefore un-medicated hyperthyroid eyes bugging out of her head, scream-ing, "Where the hell have you been? Mom has colon cancer!"

We all start crying. Except for Corinne, who keeps screaming at the tops of our heads, which are hung in shame.

When she cools down, my stepdad, Norman, walks over, and my brother, Earl, who was the man of the house between step-fathers three and two, and two and one, and one and my dad, says, "Let's fly her to Sloan-Kettering." A world-class hospital befitting my mom's station in life.

My stepdad, the current man of the house, responds, "Let's wait and see what the doctor says." And he and my brother lock angry alpha eyes.

Whereupon my brother leads my sister, Jane, and me out to the parking lot for an emergency nuclear family meeting. "He's trying to kill her," says Earl.

Corinne says, "Bastard."

I, the baby in the family, say, "What should we do?"

Jane says, "What are you talking about?"

Earl explains what's really behind my stepdad's "wait and see" attitude: "'Let's wait and see . . . until she dies and I inherit her money!'" My mom and stepdad both have winner-take-all wills, he says, making the withholding of optimal cancer care a strategic wealth-building endgame.

"Oh my God," says Jane, bursting into tears.

"I love your mom," she says before boarding the plane back to New York, after asking me to drive her to the airport. "But your brother and sister are too intense."

She doesn't know my dad.

The next morning, Jane calls from New York to check on my mom.

I tell her she's still in intensive care and that I'll call her if anything changes.

A few hours later, Jane calls again.

And then she calls again a few hours after that.

"I told you, Jane, nothing's changed, but I'll call you if anything does."

And nothing changes, including Jane, who, being Jane, calls five times a day, upsetting my family almost as much as my mom's cancer.

Then one night at dinner, after Jane calls yet again, my sister glowers at me through her unmedicated hyperthyroid eyes and says, "Can't you stop her from calling?"

I say, "I've tried."

She says, "Well, who wears the pants?"

And it occurs to me that maybe Jane does. Which triggers a dark, shameful rage that starts quietly fermenting.

Back at the hospital, my mom is finally strong enough to receive visitors, one at a time, in order of seniority.

So after everyone else has come and gone, I walk in her room and bend over her hospital bed and rest my head on her stomach, like a little boy. Maybe for the first time. Yes, I'm the baby, but I was bottle-fed—by a nanny. My mom and I aren't physically close. So I'm down there, awkwardly, and she's patting my head, awkwardly.

Then she says through her oxygen mask, "I never want to see Jane again."

I bolt up and say, "What do you mean? You said I should marry her."

My mom says, "I was wrong about Jane. She returned my Christmas present." She's sucking away on her oxygen like Darth Vader, only ghostly white instead of black.

"Earl told you?" the same Earl who told Jane that no one would ever find out.

"Earl told Corinne," says my mom—Corinne is an interrogator par excellence, having learned her craft from my dad, who was a professional interrogator of North Koreans during the war—"and Corinne told me."

"I'm sorry, Mom. But Jane never would have worn it. It's not a big deal."

My mom says, "That's just the tip of the iceberg. She's a gold digger. She came here to get her greedy little hands on my money." Which Jane and Corinne and I would all love to get *our* greedy little hands on. As would Kate, but she married the cocaine trafficker and I suspect got herself written out of the latest will.

"It was twenty-five bucks at TJ Maxx, Mom! Come on," I say. After a considered pause, during which I decide to throw us all in the ditch together, the theory being that Earl's body and mine will protect Jane's, I add, "We all returned your presents! Like we always do! Which was Earl's idea to begin with! Jane didn't even want to, until we told her it was a family tradition!"

My mom says, "You're *family.* I love you no matter what." Unless you marry a cocaine trafficker. "But I don't have to love Jane. Unless you marry her. And I hope you don't. Now please, leave me alone. I have cancer."

I leave her alone, walk back to the parking lot, and start driving around Denver, aimlessly, stunned and divided. How can I like Jane if my mom doesn't? How can I like my mom if she doesn't like Jane? And why does it matter, when I don't really like my mom?

Because I love her, and I'm the only one left in my family with the chance not to divorce. Nothing matters more to me than for my mom to see me break this terrible family tradition. Which I thought, until a few moments ago, I was going to break with Jane. (You have to get married before you don't get divorced.)

And I know Jane's no gold digger. On our first date, I hailed a cab outside her dorm. But she insisted we take a bus, because she wanted to pay her half, and she couldn't afford half a taxi.

At the time, I found that noble, but the more I think about it, I find it emasculating. I wanted to take care of her, like a man, notwithstanding that I was a sophomore cashing allowance checks from my mom. But Jane wouldn't let me be a man. Wouldn't let me be in control.

She hasn't let me be in control—now that I think about it— since the night we met!

Wait a minute! If I connect the emotional dots, if I break the family tradition of divorce by marrying Jane, *I'll continue the family tradition of men marrying women who wear the pants. Women who call when you ask them not to. Who cast you out into the emotional wilderness. Just like my mom did to my dad!*

The emasculated snake rots from the head down. *That's* how I'll redeem myself: by mixing it up with my dad! He's up at our ski house right now with Earl, in the mountains. So that's where I aim my car, like an angry homing pigeon, rehearsing the argument I'm going to have when I get there. My dad's going to say, "Jane called again," which she no doubt will have. I'm going to say, "Don't tell me I can't control her." Which I can't. "Because let me tell you something . . ." And then I'll catalog every weakness of his I can think of, rehearsing for a hundred miles of interstate highway through the Rockies.

When I get to the ski house and open the door, I see my brother, Earl, sitting on the orange vinyl couch, and my dad standing in his pajamas on the matching orange shag carpet— both of them watching TV. "Your girlfriend called," my dad says, not even giving her the dignity of a name. "She's looking for you." And I eviscerate him—from the afternoon pajamas to the afternoon TV and on and on, just as I'd rehearsed in the car. "So don't tell me Jane's looking for me." Which she is. "Asshole!"

My dad's eyes dilate as he hobbles toward me like a crazed retired bomber pilot with a bad back. Which he is. He's killed people for less than calling him an asshole. (Most of the people he bombed couldn't speak a word of English and were running away from his B-26 when he swooped down on their villages.)

That's when I notice my knee brace! From knee surgery. I was so lost in my head on the drive up that I totally forgot my body.

I hop to the opposite side of the huge black circular dinner table, trying to stay at six o'clock to my dad's twelve o'clock high as we hobble and hop around and around, my dad chasing me and screaming, "Come here, you son of a bitch!" Like he's an officer (which he is) and I'm an enlisted man in his private army (which he's told me I am) and I should obey orders, in this case to stop hopping away so that he can knock the crap out of me. Anger really does delude people into thinking strange thoughts.

My big brother rocks on the sofa, keening, "What's happening?"

Then one of the loop-filled female Velcro straps on my knee brace dangles down into the long, tapering, crushproof male fibers of the shag carpet and locks, in a reusable textile adhesive gang bang, and I trip.

My dad scoops me in a headlock and flips me on my back. He cocks his fist, his military signet ring shaking, his face twisted in rage, perhaps like it looked in the cockpit over Korea. All I can think is, All my teeth are permanent. "No one talks to me like that," he says, looking at me straight in the eyes, steadying his fist, dropping me on the shag, and hobbling off like an old grizzly.

One of my dad's few pieces of advice to me on alternate weekends growing up was, "Always think ahead of the airplane." So I tighten my Velcro straps and hop to the kitchen and grab a butcher knife *before* saying, "No one tells you you're an asshole?"

That starts my brother rocking and keening again. "What's happening?" he asks over and over.

My dad lumbers toward me. When he gets to the kitchen, he slows down, carefully aims the center of the sternum button of his pajama top, lining up the little holes where the thread goes through with my knife, until one hole locks on the tip of the blade. We're docked, female on male, plastic on steel, as he backs me up against the kitchen counter, bending me backward, until I feel the kitchen faucet pressing into my spine; there's no place to retreat. "You don't have the guts," he says. Like murder is what makes you a man—the guy who wears the pants. Which may be true, *for a bomber pilot.*

Which I'm not. I put down the knife.

Drive down to Denver.

Fly to New York.

I can't afford a phone in my dorm room. (Having observed a direct causal link between needing my mom's money and going insane, I'm trying to live on work-study jobs and student loans and grants.) So when I get back from the airport, I stop at the pay phone in the lobby and call Jane. "I don't want to see you for a while," I say.

Jane says, "Why?" She's stricken and confused.

I say, "You call too much." Which is as good a reason as any to end a two-year relationship, especially in a family where returning a sweater to TJ Maxx gets you excommunicated.

Jane says, "I call because I care."

I say, "If you cared, you'd listen, and not call." And I hang up.

Then I call my mom collect. She reminds me that she doesn't want to see Jane, either.

I hang up again, enraged, and, it suddenly occurs to me, totally alone. For about ten terrifying seconds.

Then I begin digging in my pocket for another dime. My mom might die. I almost killed my dad. My brother and sister have turned what's left of my family against the woman I'm thinking of spending the rest of my life with. Whom I just dumped. And the only person in the world I can call to help me understand what's happening to me is her.

ELEVEN

Mr. and Mrs. Right

You're in the same boat, honey.
You can't sink each other, without sinking
the relationship.
—my mom

I'm sitting on a little black couch in a little white room, next to Jane, facing Mim, our brand-new couples counselor.

Jane found Mim through a witch in the Great Pyramid in Egypt. They were drawing tarot cards together, and Jane drew the Death card, which to a witch equals transformation. To help Jane continue transforming, the witch told Jane about Mim: kind and compassionate, conveniently located in the West Village, and charges on a sliding scale, based on your ability to pay. (Nothing beats discount enlightenment.)

It's a humbling, anxious moment in the life of a couple when you admit you need a trained mental-health professional to help you get along, whether or not you ever got along to begin with. Sitting out in the waiting room before our appointment,

I couldn't help but feel sorry for myself, and for us. *What happened?*

It's not like this was a *stage* of our relationship we needed help getting through. This *was* our relationship. I had gotten used to it—to the predictable, Sisyphian suffering of it all; the devils you know, as I wrote the night I met Jane. There is comfort in knowing what lies ahead—that you will get into an argument with your partner at least once a day, usually over something minor—versus the low-grade anxiety of being in a stable, loving relationship, not knowing what the future holds. Unpredictability kills mammals—or at least drives them insane. I learned that from my lab mice in college.

Fortunately, the shame of asking for help and the anxiety of not knowing what would become of our contentious but predictable relationship was offset by a warm, cozy wave of Schadenfreude washing over me when the elevator doors opened into the waiting area of the Washington Square Institute, the institution-size counseling center where Mim works. Perhaps a dozen visibly troubled people sat scattered among the couches and chairs, flipping through magazines, staring out windows, waiting for their appointments to begin, just as we were. Then the receptionist began to call their names and they stood up, two by two, from *different* parts of the room, meeting at the passage to the institute's inner sanctum, like two tributaries converging at the self-help sluice gate. A roomful of couples who hated each other so much they couldn't sit together! If that doesn't warm your broken heart, nothing will! At least Jane and I shared the same institutional-grade sofa.

When I heard our names called, I looked up, and there stood Mim, holding a clipboard, sporting a black Betty Boop bob with bangs framing glasses that looked like a scuba mask. She looked like a cartoon character with a name to match.

We followed her through the passage between the waiting and the treatment areas, through a winding left-right, left-right labyrinth of hallways and doors to tiny soundproofed offices so vast, you didn't know whether to cry at the magnitude of human suffering or rejoice. When in doubt, I choose Schadenfreude. I congratulated myself on having escaped the gravity of this place for so long, given how many of my neighbors were already here.

We walked into Mim's tiny office, a cubicle really, plaster-boarded out of the vast loft space and which I gathered—judging by how Mim double-checked the room number on the clipboard before opening the door—had been recently assigned to us. All the therapists and patients and cubicles were assigned here, underscoring how common we were, how special we weren't. At some point in our shared history, Jane and I were each other's one and only; now we were just two more people who needed help, occupying whatever chamber was available.

Jane and I sat down on a little black tufted couch of the ilk some patients like to lie on during Freudian analysis. Mim sat in a simple wooden chair, facing us a foot or two away across the narrow cubicle, our backs to our respective walls. A box of tissues sat on the table to one side of our couch. A little white-noise machine sat on the floor, humming away. Evidently, it got loud in there, and weepy.

I think I know why. When Jane finds out that she is wrong and I am right, as confirmed by a mental-health professional

(Mim), she (Jane) is going to scream and cry. For example, for breakfast one morning Jane served slices of fresh pineapple, *without* removing the core, that little hard part in the center. "Which everyone knows is not edible," I tell Mim as the session begins.

"I don't believe in wasting food," says Jane.

"It's not *food*," I say. "It's *pig* food. That's why Hawaiians feed it to pigs." (My mom lives part-time in Maui; I know.)

"That's insulting," says Jane.

"That's the truth," I say. "*People* eat pineapple *rings*. That's why they're called pineapple rings." And then, turning to Mim, I say, "Right?"

Mim stares at us through her prescription scuba mask, its lenses so thick, you can't tell whether her pupils are magnified or dilating in horror. "This is going to take some time," she says, standing up to open the door, then adding, to herself as much as to us, "I don't know why couples wait so long to get help."

Out the door and through the labyrinth we go, past ambient murmuring and occasional sobbing and the odd scream from dozens of other unhappy couples whose sessions are running a little longer than ours—right-left, right-left through the warren of drywalled, not quite soundproof misery chambers, then into the elevator, in silence.

When the doors open, we walk to the sidewalk.

"Want to talk?" says Jane. Like men with food, women don't lose their appetite for conversation during wartime.

We walk across the street to the coffee bar, order two lattes, sit at a café table, and analyze our session. Soon we're jacked up on caffeine and Mim.

"You think she's any good?" says Jane.

"She's all we can afford," I say. Mim told us she had just been certified by her mentor to treat couples, hence the sliding scale. She's a beginner, perfect for couples with more problems than money—for example, us.

"How could Mim not see that one of us is right and the other is wrong?" says Jane. "I just don't get it." Which is another way of saying, How could Mim not see that I—Jane—am right?

"She just needs to get to know us," I say, which is another way of saying, Mim just needs to get to know you, Jane, and then she'll think what I think. "Besides," I say, "I thought she was pretty clear."

"I did, too," says Jane. Which is when the subtext bubbles its way to the surface. "Did you see the way she looked at you when you said the stuff about the pineapple rings?"

"She's afraid to say I'm right because she'll alienate you," I say.

"That's ridiculous!" says Jane.

"You're ridiculous!"

And thus the central question in our lives is now, Whose side is helmet-haired, prescription scuba mask–wearing, inscrutable, inexperienced, but affordable Mim on?

To find out, we *have* to go back for another session, like two latte-drinking lab mice fighting over the last bit of foam.

The next week, pretty much the same thing happens: Mim listens and doesn't take sides. When we're finished, she says, "See you next week." Jane and I go to the coffee bar to argue.

This goes on week after week after week.

One day, at the end of the lattes, after years of bickering over everything from whether it's insensitive of me to scrape the poppy seeds off of Jane's bagel before I take a bite to who opened the new soy milk before the old one was finished (Food perhaps being the battleground for the proxy wars over the much deeper divide of sex), Jane and I finally agree: One of us must be right about *something;* something's wrong with Mim for not seeing it. *Mim* is the problem!

So we start seeing her twice a week. Every Tuesday at four o'clock, Jane and I walk into Mim's office wanting to throttle each other, each of us determined to get Mim on his or her side. An hour later, we walk out wanting to throttle Mim for not taking sides. Just as the therapeutic effect starts wearing off and Jane and I start nipping at each other, we go back to the Washington Square Institute on Fridays at five, which medicates us for the weekend by refocusing our anger on our *common* enemy: Mim.

Mim is the best thing to happen to our relationship in years.

Every few sessions, during lulls in arguments, Mim reads a page from her textbook theory of relationships: Couples choose each other because they remind each other of home. They go with what they know, in order to finish the unfinished business of growing up, which means growing out of unhealthy childhood behavior patterns into healthy, liberated adult ones. So not only is it possible to go home again emotionally; it's impossible not to. And when couples get back home, via their relationship, they're going to suffer just like they did as children, only together and in adult proportions. Which explains why there are so many miserable people here at the Washington Square Institute, holed up in the soundproof misery chambers recessed into the drywalls of the labyrinth: Everyone who had parents is a patient!

It's a great theory, short and bleak as life itself.

Practically speaking, it means the key to understanding each other is understanding the relationship each has with his or her mother. Jane's mother rejected her; my mother doubted me. By staying together and rejecting and/or doubting each other, we get to act like children. It's a textbook case of romantic love.

If we can remember that we're not each other's mothers when we see things differently, that there are two ways to serve fresh pineapple, we have a chance of being happily in love.

All of which makes sense, until we get back home.

During one session, Mim asks whether we've done our homework: mirroring, an exercise where each of us complains to the other and then the other repeats the complaint using the pronoun *I*, as though we were trading places. It's supposed to build empathy.

But how can you empathize with someone who's *wrong*? Jane is reading from a list of complaints she's written down. I am discretely extending fingers in my lap, one for each rebuttal when it's my turn to talk. I prefer spears to mirrors.

Mim says gamely, "Let's trying mirroring now."

Jane goes first, mirroring me, repeating a complaint I just made to her. "We went on a camping trip and I wanted Jane," says

Jane, "to serve me the eggs. But Jane," says Jane, "wanted to wait to serve them together with the bacon." Just like we do at home. The bacon wasn't ready. "I was so mad she controlled my eggs that I hiked off into the woods and left Jane," says Jane, "alone by the campfire."

"Good," says Mim. "Is that what you said, James?"

It is. Perfect mirroring: my words coming out of Jane's mouth, giving me a chance to hear how I actually sound. Which is why I hate this exercise.

Now it's my turn to mirror Jane, repeating a complaint she's just made to me. "We went out for brunch, and I," meaning Jane, "didn't like my food. I sent it back. The waiter was going to throw it out anyway. So I, meaning Jane, took a few more bites before he took my plate away. And James got mad."

"Good," says Mim. "Now, Jane, how does that make you feel?"

"I hear James's judgment."

"James, is that true?" says Mim. "Are you judging Jane?"

"Of course!" I say, amazed that this is even an open question. "She's stealing food from the restaurant!"

Jane says, "I knew it! He's trying to squish my personality."

Mim says, "Stop!" Cupping her hands on her head like *she's* mirroring the guy in *The Scream*.

I say, "Stealing food is your personality?" as though Mim has asked us to keep talking.

Mim says, "Please!" Then, without warning, she tells us, "I can't help you anymore! I'm sorry!" Her palms are facing us, pushing away at the air in front of her face, at the invisible demon, while the white-noise machine on the floor in the corner whirs away uselessly, like a little white mouse being asked to guard two alley cats, the tissue box sitting on the side table, waving the white flag of surrender.

Jane and I fall silent and look at each other gravely, as though a doctor has just told us, "You're hopeless." Which she has.

Jane says, "What do we do?"

Mim says, "I don't know," and she stands up and opens her door. "Good luck."

It's a long, weird elevator ride back down to the street as it sinks in that maybe Mim has the right idea, maybe we should dump each other.

Then the Mim effect kicks in: We can't let a woman who wears a prescription scuba mask end our relationship!

Jane says, "She can't handle us. We're too intense."

I say, "Yeah, even if she'd taken sides, how could we have taken her seriously . . . with a name like Mim?"

Jane looks at me like it's love at first sight. "You know," she says, "I've been thinking that all along."

"Would you allow yourself to be called Mim after *you* got a Ph.D.?"

"You know," says Jane, "you're right!"

It's the most beautiful phrase in the English language, if you ask me. The phrase "I will have sex with you" being a close runner-up. But *power* is the ultimate aphrodisiac—and what is power if not being right?

Jane and I hold hands and walk down the sidewalk to the antique jewelry shop on the corner to window-shop for engagement rings. We've been coming here all summer long, since our first session with Mim. We thought she'd turn us into marriage material.

Jane looks in the window and smiles this really lovely "Wouldn't it be nice if we could do something a normal couple does?" smile.

I love her, I realize. I really do. So what if we don't get along? I love my mom, and we don't get along, either. Maybe Jane *is* right for me.

She was right about the pineapple. After we had the argument the first time, I ran down to the deli on the corner, only to discover that fresh pineapple is served in semicircular or triangular slices—the cores nefariously disguised as the vertex! Hiding in plain sight! The only pineapple rings you can buy in New York City are in cans, from Del Monte or Libby's. Evidently, pineapple rings are an artifact from my childhood, same as my emotional life. Once again, I had confused my present with my past.

Jane points to a ring in the window. I point to another: a white diamond that looks to be just under a karat, the weight at which getting a ring costs more than arguing about pineapple rings for a year under the supervision of a mental-health professional, even on a sliding scale.

Neither of us is ready to get engaged. But it's nice to dream. And finding a ring that we can both can agree on . . . well, that should take a long, long time.

TWELVE

Love Story

You're leaving me just when I belong
—song

When you fly to Houston from New York, things that locals take for granted can seem strange: the ubiquitous air conditioning, which is worse than the heat; the Israeli-Mexican flower stands, which make no sense based on any understanding of simpatico cultures, trade routes, or aesthetics; and Kate's hospital room—it makes *me* want to die.

I ask Kate if she'd like to go outside and get some air.

She murmurs, "Uh-huh."

I ask Becky, the nurse, for a wheelchair. Becky gets a gurney with an oxygen tank.

Together with Corinne, the three of us wheel Kate downstairs, until we come to the fountain in the marble atrium.

Like most buildings in Houston, Methodist Hospital is connected to a mall. There's a piano player here—of the ilk of the guy who worked at Corinne's wedding, playing a page from the same songbook as "Greensleeves"—and people in club chairs, drinking coffee, reading papers. Corinne whispers something to Kate. Kate whispers something back. Then Corinne talks to the piano player, and he plays the theme from *Love Story,* which Kate played every night as a teenager on the spinet in our living room. Now as then, Kate starts crying.

I *hate* that song. Just as I did as a kid, night after night after night, Kate closing her eyes and swaying on the piano bench in melodramatic rapture. Ugghh. Kate has the *worst* taste in music, till the bitter end. So after waiting what seems a not unseemly but brief amount of time, I ask Becky to lead us out of the atrium, to the light and the air . . . and the absence of the theme from *Love Story.* Becky says there's a maze of tunnels we could get lost in, and with a patient who could go into cardiac arrest at any time, that's not a good idea.

So she asks two maintenance men passing by to serve as our pathfinders, and together—there are six of us now—we wheel down a series of hallways: a compact, superefficient CCU nurse; a statuesque bottle-blond former beauty-pageant queen; two husky uniformed janitors; a prematurely gray-haired guy in a button-down shirt and wire-rim glasses; and a bald woman in a nightgown and a face mask on a stretcher. We're the musicians of Bremen, the Grimm's fairy tale where the ragtag band of musical animals makes its way to the city, gathering motley friends along the way; only we're fleeing the music, trying to find the light and air, in Houston.

Then we round a blind corner and literally run into Roger, who happens to be a drummer. The band is complete.

Kate met Roger at a bar in Maui. Her second husband, a fitness nut who filled their home with framed posters of himself bare-chested, had just left her after telling her the prospect of tampering with her chest broke his heart (the only kind of surgery he supported was plastic), which, according to Kate, came out of his mouth as the somewhat less felicitous sounding "I want you to die beautiful,"—a real step down from Kate's first husband, the convicted cocaine trafficker, who also worshipped at the temple of the body—you do a lot of push-ups in federal prison—but to his enduring credit, led Kate to the light by example: If he could quit dealing drugs, she could quit using. It was happy hour, Kate was unhappy, so she drove to the beach, sat on a bar stool, and waited for someone to buy her a drink and make her happy. Kate was nineteen years older than Roger, with one breast and a life expectancy most people would describe as "not long enough." But evidently this did not deter him. He played drums in heavy-metal rock bands, had waist-length silky black hair and Maori-esque tattoos all over his neck and torso, which did not deter her. Their physical quirks were comparable. Neither of them were put off by the fact that their scores on the verbal SAT were roughly mirror images of each other (hers was 800). They *liked* each other.

And here they are.

Here *we* are, meeting each other for the first time—Roger looking worried and angry underneath those tresses, like Sitting Bull after the cavalry attacked. "I was wondering, Where the fuck is my girlfriend?" he says. "You must be Kate's brother."

Awkward. He *is* Kate's boyfriend. Here I am, dragging her out of the hospital, potentially risking her life—what little she has left of it—without bothering to tell the guy who checked her in. But I can feel, instantly, that I am closer to Kate, more of a peer, more in tune with her needs than he is. We have history. They met at happy hour—possibly after someone else had made her happy. She *is* his girlfriend—though I am the one who bought her roses for Valentine's Day. I hug him, kind of.

We continue rolling Kate down a few more halls, passing the swinging doors into the ER and cloth-walled rooms filled with ill, injured, and suffering people. Then we go by a door that opens onto a loading dock, cross a parking lot, and take the sidewalk to a fountain—which has been turned off for the winter—covered in nonflowering, winter vines. Add in ambient noise and exhaust fumes from three million people with no mass transit, no carpooling, and at least one air conditioner in every interior space, and it's worse than the corner of Seventy-second and Broadway, because the architecture here is so bleak. But the weather is beautiful—the sun is shining, the sky is blue, and the air is warm—and Kate loves the sun on her face, so the seven of us stand there, or lie there, and bask in it, and, in my case, cry.

I have dreaded this moment for so long. Some people are afraid to put a snail in their mouths. Some wouldn't be caught dead wearing white in winter. I am afraid to be seen in tears. Yes, my sister may die. But even scarier than her death is my weakness.

But here is my sister, outside on a street corner at rush hour, having lost all her hair and much of her weight but none of her dignity. *Not* ashamed.

And I'm not ashamed. This is just the way things are. I stand there on the sidewalk, smelling the exhaust fumes, in tears, elated to be feeling something other than crippled.

THIRTEEN

Manhattan Transfer

Hard love, hard town
Our love is not easy
Our love is the sound
Of hard love in a hard town
—song, year five

After our first couples counselor fired us mid-session, Jane and I began seeing Charles, a hypergroomed, upright, fine-boned little fellow on the skeletal side, like Audrey Hepburn, only chestier. I think he worked out; he was definitely *metrosexual*. I distrusted him the instant he opened his freshly painted door. If a man had this much time to primp, what was he *not* doing? But I gave Charles the benefit of the doubt. I could get along with anybody except, it seemed, Jane. So anybody who could help me get along with the woman I loved was somebody I wanted to know.

It seemed like Charles might be the man. Week after week, he just sat there as we bickered, calm but alert, *professional*.

Then suddenly, without warning, everything changed.

Jane is complaining, like she usually does. Dissolving in tears. So far so good. Then she screams, "Don't you care about my feelings?" At Charles! Like *he's* her boyfriend.

Charles says, "Of course I care about your feelings," like he *is* her boyfriend.

Jane says, "Then why don't you tell James"—her boyfriend— "that he's wrong!" i.e. behave like a boyfriend and defend her from her boyfriend.

Charles says, "That's your experience, Jane. James may have a different experience." He's acting like a therapist—rational and impartial.

"Are you telling me *you don't believe me*?" says Jane.

Because when you're trying to win an argument, the last thing anyone wants in a therapist—or a boyfriend—is rationale and impartial.

"Of course I believe you," says Charles with great empathy, which can easily be mistaken for self-serving bias.

"Then how could you not tell James *he's wrong*?" says Jane, confusing empathy with self-serving bias, sounding like my girlfriend. "What kind of therapist are you?"

"Are you telling me how to do my job?" says Charles, sounding now like a boyfriend—of Jane's—threatened and defensive.

"Now *you're* mad at me!" says Jane, like she's the victim. "Now it's two against one!"

"I am *not* mad at you!" says Charles, audibly—and visibly— mad, his hypergroomed calmly metrosexual mien tensing from the eyes out in ripples of anxiety, like a glassy reflecting pool that's just had a stone skipped on it.

And boom! Charles and I have changed places—or he is now me anyway, as far as Jane is concerned. I've heard somewhere that this is normal in a therapeutic relationship: what mental-health professionals call transference, where a patient transfers feelings she has for one person—her boyfriend, for example—to the therapist, and then works out those feelings in a kind of role-playing. The problem is, those feelings are supposed to transfer *only* in the mind of the patient. The therapist is not supposed to really act like her boyfriend, or to look at his patient as though she's his girlfriend. Which is exactly what Charles is doing.

That is when I consider calling the health insurance company, after we get out of here, and offering to cover the session, not just the co-pay. Getting to watch my relationship as a spectator, like it's theater, with someone else playing me? That is definitely worth the price of admission.

"I am so sorry," says Jane, calm as a stone killer. "You are *totally* in denial, Charles. Are you *seriously* going to tell me you were *not* mad?"

You can see Charles's beady little third eye squinting through the darkness of his training and experience, trying to find an excuse.

It is *awkward* watching a man search for a plausible, credible lie right in front of you, having been driven first to explode by the woman sitting next to him, and then to lie to cover up his explosion. And yet it's *awesome* watching this happen, because so often that man is me. *This* is my kind of mirroring, versus that stupid exercise that our first therapist, Mim, tried to teach us to increase empathy for each other. Who needs empathy when you've got Schadenfreude? When my bubbling brook of joy at Charles's misery can numb my pain and anger? Yes, when this session is over, I'm going to have to trade places with Charles and actually live the role again. But for now, it's likc taking a vacation from my life, and watching someone else suffer it. How cool is that?

"James," says Jane, suddenly pulling me in to *their* argument. "*You* saw it. Was Charles mad?"

That's when I decide not to call the health insurance company, because Charles and I really have changed places. I am not a spectator. I am now the counselor. Which is a problem. I can't solve my own problems, much less a mental-health professional's, combined with the fact that Jane is right: Charles *is* lying. But the *last* thing I'm going to do is tell that to Jane, thereby affirming her. Any more than I can affirm Charles. They're both wrong. And I need them both to see this, and to come to a shared understanding.

"Charles," I say, as the de facto counselor to our soon-to-be-former counselor, drawing on my years of experience as a patient, "What Jane is trying to say is that she needs you to validate her feelings. I can't validate them. Because they're in opposition to mine."

"Okay," says Charles, taking my advice, "I was mad at you," he says to Jane. "I'm sorry."

"I *knew* it!" says Jane, beaming, as though it will help her romantic relationship to drive her couples counselor first to lose his temper and then to lie to conceal having lost his temper and then to reveal having lost his temper and lied to conceal it, making him an emotionally unstable liar. Which usually is not something to smile about—notwithstanding that he apologized.

"I'm human," says Charles, as though human is a good thing to be in a relationship with Jane, or with me. "But I can't validate your animosity toward James."

"An-Ni-MOSS-ity?" says Jane. "An-Ni-MOSS-ity?" she repeats, pouring more vitriol into that third syllable than you'd think it could hold—two gallons of bile in a one-gallon canteen.

"Jane," I say, jumping in to the therapeutic breach, "what Charles is trying to say is that he understands where you are coming from. But he can't take sides."

"I'm not asking him to take sides!" says Jane, which I think she is asking him to do. "I am asking him to listen to me!" And she bursts into tears.

I've never been to a bullfight. But I imagine the expression on Jane's face at that moment is not dissimilar to the expression on a matador's as he withdraws his sword from the heart of the mortally wounded beast. It's a mixture of triumph and humbling sorrow that the *strongest* creature in the arena is, in the end, weaker than the *smartest* creature; in this case, a mental-health professional with more years of higher education than the two of us combined has just had his aorta pierced by a master . . . of divinity.

"You're supposed to be a professional!" says Jane, cutting off both of Charles's ears, and then his tail. "You should have held your *boundary!*"

As for Charles's face, I'm looking into what our first counselor, Mim, might have called an emotional mirror, and seeing what it actually feels like to be me: every hair in place, above eyes that look like they've been forced wide open in a wind tunnel.

FOURTEEN

The Last Sound You Hear

Take a look, a good look
Take a look at me
Don't you mind I left behind the things I used to be?
I don't play for strangers
It's not the way it was
I spent all my magic to buy all their applause
Now most of them don't love me
Some just love me less
They still miss the magic of their almost-famous guest
Take a look, a good look
Take a look inside
Take it slow
You'll feel the glow
It's just the fire that died
—song by Kate

I'm sitting on the little wooden visitor stool next to Kate's hospital bed, holding Kate by the hand, praying to God to give us one more conversation.

The last time I saw Kate, we were at an Asian restaurant not far from here, drinking excellent red wine with our palate-destroying pad thai. (We do that in Texas.) "Don't tell my oncologist," said Kate, meaning don't report her for mixing Cabernet and chemo. As though stage IV cancer really might succumb to chemotherapy.

When, thank God, Kate opens her eyes.

"I love you," I say.

"Why didn't we do this before?" says Kate, surprised, not unreasonably, to see me sitting here, dutifully, like a loving brother, when I have been absent so long.

"Why do you think?" I say.

"Because we were both too chickenshit," she says, hitting the nail right on the cowardly head.

I love not having to reveal myself, and yet be clearly understood. It's like I'm strong and silent, even though I'm really weak and voluble. It's like talking to an angel. Kate speaks with a kind of no-nonsense, "Say what you mean today, because you may have no tomorrow" clarity, rooted in the fact that she really may have no tomorrow. *We* may have no tomorrow. Her embarrassments will die with her, very soon.

As will mine, *if* I reveal them to her. Notably the fact that I am a miserable human being, in part because I am a miserable husband with a wife I love but cannot understand, stuck in a marriage that I have no idea how to improve, or end, nor have any of the thirteen couples counselors Jane and I have seen over the years. Maybe Kate's parting gift will be to turn things around for us. Like being an organ donor for a dying couple, giving us the gift of her happy-relationship-having heart, or liver, or whatever organ it is that people who have happy relationships use to be happy. Notwithstanding that, based on my personal observations of Kate's two marriages, two divorces, dozens of boyfriends, and the occasional girlfriend, she's not any better at being happy together than I am. In fact, she may be worse. But other people's problems are always clearer than one's own, and those who can't do, teach, and I need guidance. Who better to guide me than a tequila-swilling, cocaine-loving, omnisexual nymphomaniac hilarious genius on her deathbed?

"What should I do about Jane?" I say, as though we're here to talk about me, which, at the moment, we are.

Kate looks at me through morphine-clouded eyes. "I see smoke around your head." Which may be just the morphine dilating her ocular blood vessels. Or she may be really seeing things not visible to the naked eye. Jane says she's had visions. And I believe in alternate realities—I've lived in one through thirteen marriage counselors. Maybe Kate's onto something. Maybe she's not speaking metaphorically. "You're a volcano," she says. "Something's gonna blow."

And she falls back to sleep, having predicted that something bad is going to happen to me, or something odd. (Some people don't think an exploding volcano is a bad thing. Jane has told me many times, in her "I'm not mystical, I just see things you can't see" way, that what we call "death" is just a portal to another life.)

When Kate wakes up, she asks, "Am I going to die here?"

I'm the baby of the family. I'm not qualified to have this conversation. Shouldn't my mom or Corinne be answering this question? Or a nurse? Or a doctor? Moreover, who are we to say? As grim as Kate's predicament appears to be, I don't believe she's going to die. Or I can't believe she's going to die. I'm *afraid* she's going to die, yes. But I'm afraid of a lot of things. So terror in itself means nothing to me, other than I am alive—for that is what being alive means to me: to be terrified. And who wouldn't be terrified to see their sister in a hospital bed with an IV stuck in her neck, bald, drug-addled, skeletal, drifting in and out of consciousness, with a nurse popping in occasionally, a smile on her face, like this is just another day at the office—which for a nurse in a critical-care unit, I suppose it is. Nobody's told me anything about dying, and until they do, I plan to go on living like there's a tomorrow. Living the dream. And sister, I can live it indefinitely—for years and years and years. Till the doctors and nurses die. Or the charity fund runs out. When you've run through thirteen marriage counselors, in a relationship marked by arguments since the night you met, through parts of seven presidential administrations, your capacity to hope in the face of seeming hopelessness is beyond normal human limitations. It's paranormal, like the vision Jane saw in the fog around our pond when she walked at sunrise. Who wants to believe things really are as they appear? Certainly not me.

"I don't know," I say, which seems to me an honest answer.

"I don't want to die here," says Kate, sounding suddenly serious, hopeless, and yet determined. She's going to get very little of what she really wants out of life from here on, she seems to be saying—*so make sure you listen to everything I ask for.*

"Where do you want to die?" I ask, smiling, as though I'm making dinner reservations.

"In a thousand-dollar-a-night luxury suite at the Grand Wailea in Maui, surrounded by all my family and friends."

I do the math. "If you make it out of here," I say, "I'll pay for it."

"Really?"

"Really," I say, knowing she'll probably die before I have to pull out my credit card. It's so easy to make big promises when you know you'll never have to keep them; the silver lining of love on a deathbed: You get to be a big spender and a cheapskate at the same time. Though this is one financial burden I am praying I have to bear, as I fall asleep in the reclining chair, the same kind I slept in the night before Julian was born in Jane's hospital room, drifting off to the hiss of oxygen and the morphine motorboat purr of an emaciated stage-IV cancer patient, snoozing.

I am awakened by the rustling of the night phlebotomist at 3:00 A.M., when vampires do their work.

The blood spurts out of my sister's vein into one little vial and then, after it's filled, into another, both of which the phlebotomist labels and places upright in a little plastic tray with the samples taken from other patients on the ward. What tests are going to be performed on the blood? I wonder. What information are they seeking? What could they possibly do with the information that's better than letting Kate sleep?

That's when it hits me that everyone here is afraid of the fundamental fact of life: death. There are billions of dollars of machines and medicines and manpower invested to fight it, and nothing to address it, all of us too afraid to admit she's gonna die, I'm gonna die, you're gonna die, we're gonna die. All of our relationships will end, whether they are happy or not. The only real choice we have is whether to end them—or continue them—on our terms.

"Why are you waking up a dying woman to take a blood sample?" I ask.

"Those are the rules," says the phlebotomist.

"Why can't you just let her sleep?"

"You'll have to ask the doctor."

I look at the tubes and the wires connected to Kate's neck and chest, at the bags of fluids, and at the monitors—beeping and flashing her pulse across a screen, a little green beeping, bouncing ball that means she's alive.

"Correct me if I'm wrong," I say, "but is the last sound my sister's going to hear is herself flatlining?"

The phlebotomist looks up from the little plastic tray of blood samples. "When you put it that way," she says with a smile on her face, "I guess you're right!" This is how you walk into a dying woman's hospital room and draw her blood as though it mattered: You make believe.

Just as you do when you walk into the office of a new couples counselor after the first two have told you you're hopeless.

FIFTEEN

Psycho Therapist

You get the shrink you deserve.
—an anonymous New Yorker (probably)

After things exploded with Charles, Jane and I—like many lovers who have been badly burned—descended into a psychotherapeutic wasteland of casual flings and one-hour-stands: couples counselors, sex therapists, clinical psychologists—all women, all recommended by Jane's friends, all personally vetted by Jane, and, coincidentally or not, all pretty much insane.

Starting with Jackie.

Jackie was a woman of a certain age, returning to the workforce after an extended absence—or maybe she had been absent her whole life and was joining the workforce for the first time—thanks to the training program at the Blingdale Institute, a sliding-scale quasi-school on the Upper West Side. Frail, fidgety, furtive, Jackie looked postdivorce or postchildren or, in any case, post*trauma,* and very much *pre*experience. (Just like Mim, Jackie had just been unleashed by her supervisor to begin counseling patients as part of her training. You had to start somewhere, why not with a couple who had inspired their first counselor to stand up midsession and fire them, and their second counselor to start a screaming argument?) You looked at Jackie and thought, She's visibly incompetent. Then you thought, But she is charging only fifteen dollars an hour (thank goodness for the rich trustees of the Blingdale Institute)—the price of two margaritas, which I'd need if I weren't here looking at Jackie. Let's give her a whirl.

Things started out normally enough. Jane and I argued in front of Jackie. Jackie scribbled notes on a legal pad, walked out of the room to the other side of a one-way mirror to consult with her supervisor: a voyeur with a Ph.D. Then she walked back in and dispensed her supervisor's advice as though it were her own; like Christian to Cyrano de Bergerac, only instead of protesting her love, Jackie suggested how we survive *our* love: Seek first to understand, then to be understood.

It was the same well-intentioned, useless advice we'd gotten from Mim and Charles, now more than ever a hopelessly inert bromide when mixed with the actual chemistry of our relationship: Seek first to win the argument, then console the loser. The key to our success as a couple being that neither of us ever had to do any consoling, because neither of us ever conceded defeat. (Love means never having to say you're sorry.) Ours was a house with *two* winners, *and* a discount Ph.D. (sitting on the other side of the one-way mirror). But because the advice was being delivered by a trainee instead of the Ph.D., instead of costing me five or ten margaritas per session, Jackie cost only two!

This left us enough money to spend on a weekend at a cute

little country inn run by an Austrian gourmet. One night, after a dish of awesome trout amandine and spätzle, Jane and I got into a screaming argument—over what, I cannot say. (Does it matter if the bomb's filled with plutonium or uranium?) All I know is, Jane locked herself in the cute little wooden phone booth (it was an authentic period inn) and called Jackie at home. Evidently Jackie, like Charles, did not believe in holding a boundary, in this case between her personal life and ours. The problem with this approach being that Jackie did not live with the Ph.D. whose advice she dispensed in her office. When you called her at home, she had to think for herself. And these were her thoughts: Jane should hang up and call the local police and have me checked into the local jail.

A few minutes later, Jane, sitting under the canopy of our cute little four-poster bed, agreed that this was an extreme solution to our problems, versus spending the rest of the weekend at the inn eating trout amandine and spätzle. Jane never expected Jackie to actually believe her, as most therapists are trained not to believe either party at face value.

But Jackie was not a trained therapist. She was a trainee who believed everything Jane told her at face value, inspiring the recommendation to have me arrested.

Mental-health professionals call this "identification": the phenomenon of seeing yourself in someone else, and if you are insane, well, *there you are.*

SIXTEEN

Death Becomes Me

If ever you should change your mind
If ever you find a world more fine
Just tell me, "I am leaving
I must go or stop believing in a sunny day"
If you should change your mind
—song

I'm sitting in a little windowless meeting room around the corner from Kate's windowless hospital room, seated at a round table with my mom, Corinne, Kate's boyfriend Roger, the social worker from the hospital, and the social worker from the hospice, who opens a catalog with color pictures of the Houston Hospice and hands them to me. She's like a travel agent selling a berth on a cruise ship, only this is really a cruise to nowhere.

"Wow!" says Roger, looking at the photographs of richly appointed mahogany-paneled guest rooms—or perhaps at the gurgling limestone fountain in the landscaped courtyard, one of many distinctive architectural features of a mansion that once belonged to a fabulously wealthy oil baron, until he bequeathed it to the city to use as a hospice. "That's nicer than our apartment!"

He's not kidding. He's staying in a stucco-walled "One Month Free!" studio he and Kate rented when they flew here from Maui, so she could get better cancer care than in the islands. Their apartment is in the pawnshop district—the part of town where, if you are a rock drummer (as Roger is) you can get your drums stolen and then drive a block or two and find your stolen drums for sale in a pawnshop window. It's a place so squalid, it makes you want to die, which means the prospect of dying in the hospice, at the living standard of a fabulously wealthy oil baron, is a big step up. Just the thought of it makes you feel glamorous, like Oscar Wilde, who famously remarked on his deathbed in Paris that he was dying as he lived: above his means.

The only thing wrong with this picture is that the oil baron wasn't fabulously wealthy enough—there are only twenty-two baronial chambers to accommodate the hundreds of doomed people at any given time who want to die in baronial splendor instead of in one of the $3,000-a-night steel and linoleum critical-care units equipped with $100,000 worth of state-of-the-art monitoring machines that measure your imminent demise, in real time audio and video feedback. Our only hope that Kate will escape having to hear the *beep-beep* of her still-beating heart changing to the solid ringtone that signals her heart has stopped beating is that the heart of one of the lucky twenty-two currently beating at the hospice stops beating before Kate's does, allowing us to move Kate over there.

I read somewhere about an experiment where nuns prayed

for women to get pregnant and, by doing so, actually raised the birth rate by a statistically significant margin, way beyond chance. Or maybe Jane told me about it. Either way, if prayers can help life begin, it seems to me prayers can help life end. I've never heard of a system where you don't get the bad with the good. That's the story of my life; it's a package deal. People pray for other people's demise all the time—in war, in sports, in politics, and, today, in the Houston Hospice.

"Dear God, I hate to trouble you with what less enlightened souls might consider a ghoulish request, but please visit the Houston Hospice and free up a bed for Kate. Ideally a bed with someone old in it, someone who's led a full life and has had the chance to say good-bye to his or her loved ones—and vice versa. It's not that Kate's life is worth more than anyone else's; it's that *mine* is. I need to get her out of here and in there, to feel good about myself. Because I'm gonna be here after she's gone. So please, God, if I have any favors to ask in the favor bank, please use one for Kate."

A few hours later, the social worker appears in the CCU and says a bed has opened up in the hospice; Kate can move in today.

Chance? *Perhaps.*

Either way, I wonder whom God called home: young, old, woman, man?

But I don't wonder very long. Because I'm ecstatic my sister won't be dying here. It's not Schadenfreude—happiness in the face of another's sorrow. But I cannot imagine being happier than I am right now, and the reason I am happy is that somebody died! It's unseemly, really. But some of the best things in life are.

"It's not the Grand Wailea," I tell Kate when she wakes up and I explain that she's going to move to a room far nicer than this. "But it does cost five hundred dollars a night."

"Anyplace is better than here," she says, sounding resigned for the first time.

Soon the two of us are riding in the back of an ambulance, Kate on a stretcher, me on a bench, looking out the window, *measuring*. Seeing, for the first time, that life is not infinite, not part of a continuum, not before, not after, but right now, always right now, and therefore never again: This is the last ride in an ambulance for my sister (when you have a heart attack in a hospice, they don't take you to a hospital); this is the last time a medical professional—in this case, a paramedic—will try to save my sister's life (the whole point of going to a hospice alive is to get wheeled out dead); this is the last time Kate will think that she is anywhere but at a hospice. I've yet to use the word in front of her.

We hit a little speed bump—one of many on the crosswalks in Medical Oz to prevent *additional* patients from having to check in—bouncing Kate awake. "Where am I going?"

"To a fabulous mansion."

"Am I going to die?"

"We're all going to die, Kate. Some sooner than others."

"Am I ever going to get better?"

"I don't know," I say. "But I'll tell you this: If there's anyone

in the world who can survive what you have, and I don't know
that there is, but if there is, that person is you."

I mean it. Because . . . who knows? Who am I to say what
she is and is not capable of? Kate has the energy of ten people
and has had more lives than any of the many cats she's survived.
In the process, she has extended the boundaries of what I
thought humanly possible, many times. I have seen her cater
her own wedding for 250 guests, on three hours of sleep and a
hangover, scooping out frozen New Zealand lobster tails like
she's popping roasted peanuts from a shell, the tails so hard
and encrusted, they made my fingers bleed. I have seen her
reading a paperback at three in the morning like it's three in the
afternoon of any other day, except she's just eaten the same
magic mushrooms that have me and my pre-Jane girlfriend hal-
lucinating, retching, and calling the poison-control center. She's
opened for the Beach Boys and Steve Miller, and had her face
crushed by a psychotic European boyfriend and reconstructed
in London a few weeks before landing in New York and re-
painting my apartment. She's lost at least one breast to a surgeon, then subsequently lost one husband, and then found
herself a new thirty-year-old boyfriend during happy hour on
the beach. She's a freak. A brilliant force of nature. She's forty-
eight years old. Who am I to say that's all you get?

We turn and drive through iron gates attached to brick columns, each holding a brass plaque with the word HOSPICE. I've
never seen that word, it occurs to me looking out the ambulance
window, anywhere near an actual hospice; the word *hospice*
being different from *hospital*—especially when you are driving

into one. I squint to blot out the *s* and the *i* and the *c*. So the plaque reads HOPE. The power of positive blinking.

I look on the bright side: This is an answered prayer. This is what I wanted. If Kate weren't on a morphine drip, she would want it, too; she would understand just how lucky she is to be here, and she would thank me. We have just left a place that tries to keep you alive at literally any cost, a place where death is the ultimate failure, to come to a place where death is success. *This* is why you come here—to succeed! Freeing up the bed for the next doomed patient is a mark I can hit, I think, as the paramedics open up the back doors and wheel Kate out. I can help my sister die with alacrity.

Saying good-bye, moving on, accepting that things must end: It's not my strong suit. I've been to thirteen marriage counselors. And the last twelve sounded a lot like the first one: I can't help you; go home and get your affairs in order; your marriage is terminal. And of course there were a few individual therapists along the way, all of whom I had trouble leaving, too. After all, things might get better the next visit.

But I didn't endure my childhood to give up now. I didn't grow up with a father who left when I was five and, when I did see him, gave me two choices: Believe his dim view of life, or retreat into my own magically optimistic vision of possibility.

My brother, Earl, has a wooden placard on his office wall: NEVER, NEVER, NEVER GIVE UP. Since this plaque is in Earl's office, the quote is attributed to Donald Trump, instead of Winston Churchill. Nevertheless, it's the thought that counts. How many happy memories of life with Jane do I have that have taken place between failed marriage counselors who told us to give up?

How many happy memories would I not have had, had I believed them and given up?

The games we played in her seminary room when I was an
undergraduate, like Pass the Rabbit: sitting on a floor in a circle
with the other M.Divs, holding her hands up to her head, thumb
in each ear, twinkling her fingers while bugging out her eyes
and tightening her lips like a trumpet player, trying to make the
other students laugh first. Jane was so free, so happy, like a
child, and I felt free and happy to be with her.

Our first trip to Paris, to the cheapest hotel we could find in
the Sacre Cour: an honest-to-goodness straw mattress, real crois-
sants and jam for breakfast, walking the streets and gardens for
hours holding hands, Jane sharing her deepest love, Europe,
with me.

The mountain bike she bought for my birthday and set in
our tiny apartment, festooning it with balloons and a giant
glitter-filled card. I hadn't felt that way since I was a boy, and
maybe not even then.

Jane getting up at three in the morning to make me hot tea as
I pulled all-nighter after all-nighter at my desk, learning how to
be a speechwriter, a kind of alchemy that transformed my solitary suffering into the shared sacrifice of building a life together.

The morning we slept late in Venice and the chambermaid
knocked on our door and, nervous she would disappear before I
made arrangements for her to come back and clean our room, I
opened up, wearing only a towel and not speaking Italian, held
up two index fingers and rubbed them together to mean *come
back at two* as opposed to *eleven*, which, judging by the chambermaid's dilating eyes she understood to mean *ménage a trois?*

Sending her literally running down the hallway, which set Jane laughing in bed.

Visiting Maui, Jane joining Kate in enticing my mom to throw septuagenarian caution to the wind and kick off their sandals and splash through the fountains at the fancy hotel as I photographed them.

The transcendent gift of my children—transporting me to an emotional continent I didn't even know existed.

They're like photographs, these memories and thousands more—many *are* photographs—and I cannot imagine anyone else in them but Jane.

Perhaps I would have different happy memories with a different woman if I had left Jane? This is a thought many of my therapists have asked me to consider—before I left *them*.

I really meant it when I said, "Till death do us part." And as much as I have wished in our darkest hours . . . days . . . *years* for God to get me out of here, he hasn't. Here we are, a deal is a deal.

When Oprah Winfrey came out with her magazine, I recall the lead article was entitled, "You *Can* Change Your Mind." What an amazing idea, I thought. I could just walk in the house and tell Jane, "I know I said 'Till death do us part,' but Oprah says I can change my mind." Granted, Oprah's not married. But she looks a lot happier than I do.

I once asked my father, "Why did you ever get married to Mom?"

He said, "One word."

I was thinking, *Sex.* Or maybe *pregnant,* in case he'd already gotten sex. Or *money,* as my mom came from a wealthy family.

He said, "Duty."

"Duty?"

"I gave her my word, son. And you've never known me to lie."

In fact, I had known him to lie. But reminding him that he was like every other human being was not helpful if I wanted to find out why he'd married my mom. So I kept my mouth shut.

He said that, when he was a twenty-six-year-old air force pilot, flying General Eisenhower around a few years after World War II had ended, *my mom had proposed* that they get married. He said he was too young to get married, had too much to do, too many places to go. She, having an instinctive grasp of his fidelity to the concept of duty—if not to women—said that if his commanding officer thought it was a good idea for them to get married, would he agree? His commanding officer would never endorse such an idea, he said, but if so, then yes.

Soon afterward, the commanding officer came over for dinner and, as they did in those formal, dress-for-dinner days after the war, proposed a toast: "To Captain Braly. Who's more of a fool than I think he is if he doesn't marry that girl."

"You married her because of *that*?" I said.

"I had to, son. I said I would. It was a matter of honor."

In other words, "I was just following orders." What an excellent system! It allows you never to ask, What do *I* want? Therefore, you never have to take responsibility for your personal life. It's always someone else's fault. Which is an utter *lack* of duty—because there is no responsibility to yourself.

I'm my father's son. I've got *The Soldier's Guide to Marriage* hardwired. I've asked Jane many times for permission to get divorced. She has said no many times. And so I've remained committed. Following orders. Ignoring myself. Putting duty ahead of happiness.

Here at the hospice, up is down and down is up. You literally get a gold star for abandoning ship. They hang a little placard on your door handle, covered in stickers of shiny stars and butterflies, so anyone who might walk in knows you're dead.

As the paramedics wheel Kate down the linoleum foyer, into the elevator, and out on the second floor, then down the huge baronial hallway, I am filled not with terror, but with relief: This is where life and love aren't meant to last forever.

SEVENTEEN

An Immodest Proposal

I told Mother, "If you were a black widow, you'd have eaten your children. Everything that comes out of your mouth is spiders and snakes."
—Kate

I'm sitting on a little wooden visitor stool in room 202, next to the hospital bed, holding my sister Kate by the hand, telling her how much I love her. Over and over. Like a mantra. Like the prayers I imagine those nuns prayed in the science experiment to get women pregnant. The theory being that if God hears my prayers, sees how much I need my sister, he'll throw a rope down into the abyss and save Kate from the storm by starting some miraculous, inexplicable cellular reversal deep inside Kate's organs, and we'll all go home together.

Kate is lying on her back in the bed in a white cotton nightgown and an oxygen mask, hooked up to an IV, which is connected to a motorized drug pump that she holds in her other hand, like a true believer holding a rosary. Every ten minutes, it injects Kate with Dilauded, a painkiller so powerful that the nurses wouldn't give it to her in the hospital. Evidently, Dilauded—like the hospice itself—is one of those things you get when there is no longer any reason to be afraid of dying. When dying is what you're *supposed* to do.

The hospital was filled with beeps and machines and people trying to keep Kate alive; the hospice is very peaceful and quiet. The only sounds you hear are the *hiss* of oxygen and, every ten minutes, *Zzzt* from the drug pump. Followed by *ahhh,* if Kate happens to be awake, as she is now, looking out there, through faraway Dilauded eyes.

Then she turns to me, lifts her oxygen mask, and says, "Do you love me enough to trade places?"

Like anyone on a deathbed, or standing near someone who is, I go through the five stages of grief:

1. Denial. (I can't believe Kate just asked me that.)
2. Anger. (I can't *believe* Kate just asked me that!)
3. Bargaining. (I'll tell her, "I love you, if she won't tell me," "You're lying.")
4. Depression. (She'll know I'm lying.)
5. And finally, acceptance. (I don't love anyone that much. Apart from my two little boys, Julian and Francis. And maybe Jane, on good days.)

But apart from my wife and children, I do love Kate more than anyone I've ever known. I want her to know that, and somehow to feel comforted by my conditional love in the face of a seemingly insurmountable challenge that I wouldn't take on for her, even if I could. (And when you're getting shots of Dilauded every ten minutes, anything seems possible.) So I start crying, not knowing what to tell her.

Then it hits me.

"Well," I say. "Would you want to be married to Jane?" Would you want to trade places with *me,* and be the husband to a militant organic-eating, home-birthing, placenta-freezing, self-weaning full-time mom of a wife? Who is therefore always home, whenever you are, breast-feeding—her four- and six-year-old boys—on what used to be your bed?

As a rule, I don't like to pat myself on the back. On the contrary, I'm much more comfortable hurting myself. Self-flagellating, which I like to think of as humility, is my thing, not masochism. But the moment I hear this proposed role reversal coming out of my mouth, I realize the dark genius of it. Using Kate's perception of my life to mask the fact I don't love her enough to take on her life, thus preserving the appearance of an unconditionally loving brother . . . no wonder she loves me! "Think of what you're saying, Kate. You want to trade places with that?"

Kate sucks in a hit of oxygen and considers my proposition, then takes off her mask. "When you put it like that," says Kate, "I don't think so." And she starts laughing, then coughing; then she closes her eyes and falls back to sleep. She would rather die than be me.

I feel that way too sometimes, when I think about my marriage. Arguing with Jane is like having Tantric conflict, a level of discord I've never felt before. Except when I visit my family, all of whom have gathered here in Houston to be with Kate.

My family hasn't sat in a room together in forty years, since my parents were divorced when I was a little boy. And if Kate's boyfriend, Roger, didn't have her medical power of attorney, using it to quarantine them in a little room down at the end of the hall, they probably wouldn't be sitting together now. It's a development that is both sad and quietly amusing, as I am the youngest in the family and therefore theoretically the least deserving of the privilege to be able walk back and forth between Kate's room and the family room with updates. I'm like a nerd who somehow got on the guest list at Studio 54, periodically stepping outside to update his worthier buddies who are freezing on the sidewalk on the other side of the velvet rope. *It sure is nice to have power.* The hospice director believed Roger's argument that everyone in our family except me has a toxic effect on Kate's health (notwithstanding that she's expected to die in the next few days of metastatic breast cancer), and therefore they should be quarantined—precisely the kind of medical judgment that medical powers of attorney were designed to facilitate. My mom, understandably, became enraged that she was being treated like a toxic substance, and could not walk into her dying daughter's hospice room without permission, and she demanded an emergency meeting with the hospice director, where my mom's minister joined her in a show of spiritual power. Her minister ministers to the former president Bush as well as to my mom, so the thinking was, the hospice director would see that my mom was too important to quarantine. Instead, what the hospice director saw was a woman asking, "Are you really going to listen to that Aborigine?"

So the gang's all here, in the family room, sitting on wing chairs and stuffed sofas in what used to be the mahogany-paneled study of the Tudor mansion of the oil baron who had such a nice time living here that he bequeathed it to the city of Houston as a nice place to die.

There's my father, a decorated bomber pilot, who has transferred his ferociousness from North Korean bombing runs to the ice-cream aisle in his local supermarket. "In the end," he once told me, in a pontificating moment on the meaning of life and (like many moments with him) death, "Every animal wants to crawl back to its cave to die." And though he has lived around the country and the world for much of his life, his cave is in the Deep South, near a Piggly Wiggly, a supermarket chain that evidently excels at the "Buy One, Get One Free" marketing strategy that has supersized America from the belly up. Which has transformed my dad from a lean pilot frequently bumped off flight duty for being underweight to a large landlubber in a wheelchair. The amazing thing is, he still looks sharp. There's just more of him to look at—like a top banana ballooned to a banana split on wheels, dressed in a mustard-and-brown houndstooth jacket with brown suede elbow patches, dark brown dress shirt, and mustard pants, his face hidden behind brown mirror sunglasses and a week's worth of beard. My mom says he looks like a mean, bloated snake with two little slits for eyes. But I think that's the divorce talking, that he's still brutally handsome, and that— gallons of Piggly Wiggly "Buy One, Get One Free" vanilla bean notwithstanding—the medications he's been taking for unspecified aliments have inflated him to steroid proportions, as well as blown out his color receptors, yielding a sartorial style that is blowing out mine.

My birdlike mom, his first ex-wife, is wearing the brand-new face she gave herself for her seventy-fifth birthday. I remember flying down to see it a few weeks before she unwrapped it. Which upset both of us. Looking at her as she sat at the head of the table of her mother-daughter (or, as Kate might have put it, widow-witch, for the daughter my mom shared it with was Corinne, not Kate) maintenance-free town house a week or so after the surgery, her face a gauze-wrapped, swollen blue contusion with an area marked by lipstick and normal-colored ears, I asked her what the surgeon actually did, and, more important, *why* she let him do it. This made her mad. Wasn't it obvious, she said, the cosmetic benefits of a surgical procedure that made her look as though she had volunteered to be thrown through the windshield of a car? It was not obvious, I told her. I thought she looked fine the last time I'd seen her, before the auto accident. So she put her index and middle fingers under her neck, where what she called her "waddle" evidently used to be, and flicked back and forth through the now-empty space like she was playing air harp. This tight-necked seventy-five-year-old— snipped facial muscles notwithstanding—managed to force a cunning lipsticked smile through her bandaged bruises as she contemplated the postrecovery reaction to her new face by the woman she called "poor sister," a semi-ironic moniker for her identical twin.

Aunt Jenny, who, far from poor, is loaded (having married up more times than down in roughly inverse proportion to my mom) *loaded* (she travels with her own vodka), and, as we said in high school, a load—a gigantic muumuu-wearing formerly identical twin—is sitting in the family room wearing her old face. My mom and Aunt Jenny look like a *Before* and *After* poster for plastic surgery and liposuction. One physical advantage Aunt Jenny retains are her intact facial muscles, which enable her to flash a warm and wicked southern smile, like honey that soldiers put on POWs' private parts in prison camps before releasing the red ants. My mom's efforts in that direction may be lipsticked, but her grin is tight, clipped, and sharp as a surgeon's scalpel.

My big sister, Corinne, who runs a makeup shop called Facade, without irony, and without fear, is also here. She has read *The 48 Laws of Power* at least forty-eight times and is nothing if not a positive thinker. When I pointed out that a lot of people might think Facade means superficial, Corinne replied, "They are not my customers."

Then there's my big brother, Earl, who as a teenager held a charter subscription to *Mafia Magazine,* allowing him to explain for my second-grade edification the short life and bloody death of the gangsters Crazy Joey Gallo (rubbed out in a corner booth of Umberto's Clam House in Little Italy) and Albert Anastasia (dead on the floor of the barbershop at the Park Sheraton Hotel after his last shave).

And finally there's me, the gray-haired baby brother and ambassador to Kate's boyfriend, Roger, who the men in my family call "Long Hair" and the women call "the Moron" and everyone calls "the Aborigine"—because he's a longhaired moron from Australia.

Roger suddenly rushes into Kate's room, passes me on the visitor's stool, goes over to her bedside, grabs her by the shoulders, and starts shaking. "Wake up!" he says. "Wake up, Rabbit Girl!"

Hearing a tattooed troll's pet name for my sister makes me want to vomit. It's somehow more sickeningly, taboo-shatteringly intimate than watching her have sex. I've seen *that* before. But "Rabbit Girl"? *Ick.*

However, vomiting in a hospice room is just bad form—unless you're the patient, *or* you're wearing formal lace gloves, which gives you the veneer of respectability, as was the case last night with "Princess Grace": Kate's omnisexual heiress benefactor, friend, lover, drug buddy, and (if you believe my mom's sexual conspiracy theory) rival for Roger's affections. For all I know, it could be true Kate and Grace have shared boyfriends before, possibly at the same time—as well as enjoying each other, *and* one-on-one, partaking of one's father and the other's brother. Roger—I've only known him two days, so this is just a hunch—is out of his mind. Who else but a lunatic or a saint would move in with a postmastectomy terminal cancer patient almost twenty years older than he is whom he met on the beach in Maui at happy hour? (Saints generally don't go to happy hour.) Grace flew in from London last night to say good-bye to Kate, but she said hello at dinner to too many margaritas, some of which came foaming up through her lace-covered fingers in the hall outside Kate's room a few hours later. If not for the sound of Grace retching—a low, sudden monosyllable that she tamed with the ruthless dispatch of a British soldier putting down a colonial insurrection before it could grow—I would have thought she had the hiccups; she was *that* nonchalant, even dainty. She just said, "Oops." Like she'd dropped a cocktail peanut on the floor instead of regurgitated cocktails in a hospice hallway, and she ducked smoothly into the bathroom. It was an awesome display of decorum layered over degradation: Facade, in the grandest sense—seemingly part of the very *fine* woodwork.

Grace is sitting here *right now* on the mahogany-wainscoted tufted window seat, doing a crossword puzzle with complete focus, as though taking an exam. Hungover, jet-lagged, yet impeccably groomed, she's utterly unflappable while her dying friend gets shaken awake by a drummer with more tattoos than the Illustrated Man and longer hair than Cousin It.

Kate opens her eyes and smiles.

Roger says, "I got the license! We're gonna be married!"

Kate says, "When?" sounding as surprised as I am. Only (unlike me) Kate has a shock-softening drug pump full of Dilauded jacked into her jugular vein. *Zzzt.*

"Tonight!" says Roger. "At ten o'clock!"

They hug.

Kate falls back to sleep.

Roger turns to me and says, "Just so there won't be any misunderstanding." Meaning he'll be Kate's legal next of kin. Giving him legal control over family heirlooms in their apartment: china, silver, paintings that they boxed up and flew with them here to Houston after they finally said good-bye to their hopes and dreams and lives in Maui; heirlooms that evidently Corinne thinks belong to her. "And if Corinne wants to have me arrested . . ." begins Roger—which she does. She's threatened to call the sheriff and tell him Roger is in possession of *stolen property,* Corinne's term for valuable things my mom gave to Kate when my mom should have given them to Corinne. "It's gonna be about a lot more than the silver," says Roger. "If she doesn't leave me alone, I'll kill her. I will step on her head, mate." (You can take the drummer out of Australia . . .) "I will step on her head. I'm over it!"

That's the same expression Corinne uses when *she's* reached the boiling point! All that rises really does converge.

Roger rushes out of the room.

Princess Grace looks up from her crossword puzzle and asks calmly, with a vaguely affected British lilt, like post-London Madonna, "How do you spell *wreaking,* as in 'wreaking havoc'?"

Kate says, "W-R-E-A-K-I-N-G. Wreaking." Like she's at a spelling bee. Eyes closed. Yet awake. A testament to her phenomenal drug tolerance, and to the fact she earned the highest score on the verbal SAT in the history of Colorado Academy.

We all laugh.

Kate falls back to sleep.

Grace moves to the next clue.

I sit on the stool, amazed and torn between gratitude and respect for marrying one sister, animosity for threatening to kill the other sister (though violent hyperbole does run in the family), and awe and admiration for being willing to kill to get *in* a marriage. When I've been dying to get out of a marriage since before I got into it.

EIGHTEEN

You've Got to Hide Your Gut Away

Jane: You just want alienated sex, with women you don't know, and who don't know you.
James: If that were true, we'd be having sex all the time!
—year seven

I am sitting on my suitcase in the main train station in Rome, next to Jane, who's sitting on hers, one of us holding *Let's Go Europe,* the other holding Fodor's *Europe,* trying to agree where to go next. Jane and I once disagreed for an hour over whether an Oriental rug is called an Oriental carpet or an Oriental carpet is called an Oriental rug. So agreeing where to travel for the final seven precious, expensive vacation days and nights away from New York City, while sitting at perhaps the busiest train station in Europe, full of trains leaving for virtually every destination, any of which is as appealing as any other destination, represents a degree of difficulty that we may not overcome until all the trains pull out.

Jane says she'll go anyplace. "It just needs to be sunny." She's half German, and the cloud density in the German atmosphere and therefore the German soul is so great that they need sunlight so badly, they are willing to invade countries willy-nilly to get it. "Just make a decision!"

Which reveals the secret I've been hiding from myself (but that Jane already knows) all morning, all my life: I can't make a decision. I need to go to the *right* place, and I'm terrified of going to the *wrong* place. So whenever Jane suggests someplace, I suggest someplace else, because I can see something wrong with every place.

It's a gift, my infinite capacity not to decide, and I bring it along with me everywhere I go. Because one thing I am sure of: If you make no decision, you can't make the *wrong* decision. You may die on your suitcase in the main train station in Rome, but that's better than dying in the wrong town.

Or marrying the wrong person. We've been together seven years, Jane and I, long enough to make a commitment—she thinks. But I think we need a little more time, just to make sure that what we're doing is right.

All the lights on the departures board are blinking.

The guy on the public-address system keeps announcing "*Partenze!*" over and over.

Jane's up on her feet, screaming at me, "Make up your mind before all the trains pull out!"

I am hypnotized by a flower-print dress I've caught sight of about ten feet away, fluttering in the breeze each time a train pulls out of the station—which at this point is every few minutes—

hanging off of what may be the most beautiful woman I have ever seen, who's standing next to her almost-as-beautiful friend.

Jane says, "Are you *looking* at those women?"

I look down before looking up. "Where?"

"Right there!" she says. "In the flowered dresses. Do you think they look *interesting*?"

This could be a trick question. When in doubt, choose indecision. "I don't know," I say.

"Well I do," she says. "And maybe they're going someplace interesting. Someplace we might want to go. You know, I think I'll ask them."

I want to say, "Not a good idea. Not that I plan on having sex with them. I just like to think about having it, secretly, without reality intruding. *That's the whole point of a secret*: It lives in darkness and never sees the light, like mold, my own personal private mushrooms of forbidden longing. If I had actual sex with another woman, I'd have to lie to Jane, and I can't lie to Jane because I love her. So I'd have to tell her that I had sex with another woman, and she'd leave me, and I'd end up having sex with the other woman, but not having the arguments with Jane that make me feel I belong. Because that's what it means to belong: to be with someone you love so much, you argue over everything, including not having sex.

Suddenly, Jane is over *there*, talking with the girls in French, then pointing at me, leading them back, introducing us.

"James, this is Claire," says Jane of the conventionally beautiful girl. "And her sister France." Who has a face off a French BUY WAR BONDS! poster. (I saw one in the Musée d'Orsay during our visit to Paris.) To look at her makes you want to invade.

And I'm looking at her. *"France?"* I say. "Like the country?"

"I was born in England," she says, "when my father was on sabbatical," pronouncing all the *a*'s softly, as in *ahh,* in a French-accented, English boarding school lilt that combines the best of both worlds, crème brûlée served at afternoon tea, which would be right about now. We've been at the train station since shortly after breakfast. "He didn't want any of that puritanical *merde* rubbing off on me," she says. "So he named me France."

As if to underscore that she's no puritan, France pulls out a cigarette and leans in, expecting me to light it, like a lever presenting itself to a mouse in a Skinner box. Only unlike a mouse, which would strike furiously at the lever in the hopes of hitting the random sequence that will unlock the food pellets before he starves to death and/or goes insane, I realize my chances of being rewarded for striking the match are good. France says, "Thank you," pronouncing the *a* as in *ahh* as she did before, but which in this context—reading between the lines—is an orgasmic simulacrum disguised as gratitude; code for "This is how I sound in bed: *aaah.* And rest assured, if I let a Marlboro Light into my body, I'll let you in, too. You are no more toxic than a cigarette."

It's amazing, really, how well you can read another woman's mind when you haven't seen another woman's body in two presidential administrations. This is the curse of the faithful man: the ability to see the future paired with the inability to act on the vision. This is how Cassandra must have felt, across the Adriatic. I am Cassandro. I know France wants me, but I can't do a thing about it.

Jane says, "Guess what? France and Claire are going to Positano." It's one of the numerous fishing villages we've debated
traveling to. "What do you say we all travel together?"

Had you been walking through the main train station in
Rome just then, you would have seen four suitcases placed in a
circle: standing behind two of them, a pair of achingly beautiful
twentysomething French sisters in flower-print dresses with
tortoiseshell combs in their flowing dark hair, holding matching
Michelin Green Guides; standing behind another, a beautiful
blond Ingrid Bergmanesque half German in a flower-print dress
holding Fodor's; and behind the fourth, an American man in
blue jeans and a white oxford button-down shirt holding *Let's
Go,* feigning indifference at the most exciting piece of sexual
news he has heard in eight years.

"Okay," I tell Jane. "If that's what you want."

Suddenly, France and I are on the same vacation:

Running to the train to Naples.

Lighting so many cigarettes along the bumpy way down that
my pink lab mouse fingertips are scorched yellow by the time we
arrive.

Sitting on a hydrofoil across the bay to Positano.

Pulling our suitcases through the ancient cobblestone streets.

Checking into the same hotel—neighboring rooms—with the
plan to change into our swimsuits and meet on the beach.

I haven't seen myself in a swimsuit since the last time I went
to the beach, last summer. Looking in the hotel room's mirror, I
can see things have changed since then. A little Italian bakery

opened up around the corner from my office—I'm a corporate speechwriter—and I've been going there four or five mornings a week, having apricot bear claws for breakfast: my second-favorite dessert. So now there are two little bear claws bubbling up over my waistband.

Whose *insane* idea was it to take a beach vacation looking like . . . *me*? It's one thing for Jane to see my bear claws. We have an unspoken Mutual Decay Contract; we're atrophying at roughly the same rate. But I don't have that deal with France. There's no way she's seeing the claws.

When we meet on the beach, the girls are in French bikinis and I'm in my swimsuit and button-down shirt from the train ride, like I forgot to undress the top half of myself.

Since this is Italy, the cradle of civilization, each of us has our own civilized chaise lounge, allowing Jane, Claire, and France to conveniently lay down their beach towels and beach bags, peel off their beach wraps, and wade in to the water. While I relax on mine, looking *out there,* at the horizon, like a sentry scouting for Greek invaders. (The one thousand ships that Helen's face launched set off not far from here three thousand years ago.) Like I am on business.

A few minutes later, France strolls back, dripping like a Bond girl, like Ursula Andress. I am James *not* Bond: both shaken *and* stirred by the sight of France sitting on her chaise lounge next to mine, patting herself with her towel between her bikini bottom and top, asking perhaps the most obvious and certainly the most reasonable question one traveler could ask of another while seated along the Mediterranean: "Do you not swim?"

"Of course I swim," I say, speaking the truth, then adding (all great lies are built from the truth up), "*indoors.*"

"*Indoors?*"

"I burn easily." If the measure of a man is grace under pressure, in times like these, I'd have sex with myself if I weren't already having it.

"Try this," says France, handing me a tube of sun cream. "It's very effective. It's *French.*" She says this in that cool, arrogant, *French* way—like she's an explorer in the Congo offering quinine to a savage.

I study the tube like my life depends on it, which it does. I've got one crack at masking my true self (an insecure would-be philanderer) behind the appearance of a secure, loyal *man.* "I can't," I say, pointing to the ingredients (*oxy* this, *poly* that— Greek, the language of the face that launched a thousand ships). "I'm allergic." (Real men know their limits.) I hand it back.

And there are six more days to go.

Whenever someone suggests going to the beach, I suggest a cultural monument: the hanging gardens of Ravenna; Etruscan ruins; Mount Vesuvius. "We can go to the beach anytime, girls. But how often do we find ourselves in the cradle of civilization?"

The French love civilization: France and Claire each have their own Michelin Green Guides, which rate the cultural high points of the region, from no stars to three. And the Germans admire both the French and civilization. In fact, Jane had already put her own star on the page in *Let's Go Europe* with directions to the grotto where the ancient matriarchal fertility cult castrated their male supplicants. (If you ever go there, you'll see the Italian parks department has tried to sugarcoat the history with a benign sign: a "Here lived . . ." kind of thing that you might see at a Civil War battleground. Then you realize, people got their balls cut off here, in a world without anesthesia or knife sharpeners, and you could swear you hear screams echoing through the millennia.) Six days and one castration grotto later, we're all about as white and pasty from the neck down as when we stepped off the hydrofoil.

Finally, it's our last night together. We have a little farewell dinner at a seaside trattoria, then take a farewell walk along the beach to say our good-byes. Everyone's feeling a little misty that our new vacation relationship is coming to an end . . . except me. I can't wait to go home.

Then France says, "Does anyone want to go swimming?"

Relatively modest Claire, her sister, says, "We don't have suits."

Fearless, guileless, Germanic Jane says, "That's all right with me. And I'm sure James wouldn't mind."

Which is half true (like everything in my life), the other half being I *would* mind: Seeing what you can't touch is equal parts pleasure and pain.

Off go the dresses, and suddenly the three of them are standing in the moonlight in panties and bras, which are very different than swimsuits. France's are translucent chocolate brown lace. Her skin is the color and the volume of whipped cream. She looks like a profiterole—my *favorite* dessert. It is agony to keep my eyes open, but there's no way I'm going to close them.

Then the three of them run down the beach and into the water, laughing and splashing and finally disappearing beneath the surface.

For a moment, everything's quiet—just the Mediterranean currents lapping the ancient rocks, and me, hyperventilating, looking out at the horizon, this time with genuine purpose.

One by one, their heads pop up and they start calling at me.

"James!"

"Come in!"

"You'll love it!"

Like three sirens in the moonlight, who actually used to live in Positano—three thousand years ago.

It kind of looks like fun. So I take off my shoes and socks and pants and lay them on a beach chair, then stand behind the seat back and (finally, after seven days!) unbutton my shirt and unthread my arms, so the white oxford-cloth button-down just hangs there like a little beach poncho. When France dives down again, I flick it off on the seat back and rush in . . . to water that's touching France.

It's thrilling. Every time she moves I can feel her enveloping me in currents undulating in the shape of her body. She probably thinks she's just swimming, the way women in water generally do. Just as she probably thought she was blithely enjoying an innocent scoop of mango *sorbetto* a few days ago, when we took a day trip to the island of Capri, and we all sat in the sun in the town square, licking our cones. I was reading between the pornographic lines then, just as I am reading now. I like this story.

Jane, however, is cold; she has bad circulation. Which always used to bug me.

Claire is cold, too.

But France is fine.

I just got in.

We're all vacation buddies.

Jane and Claire walk back to the hotel.

Leaving France and me alone, finally—in the dark, in our underwear, in our twenties, in the Mediterranean, where—according to *Let's Go Europe*—they invented the word *philander,* and, more important, where France and I can have sex without her seeing my body.

We swim around for a little bit, trying to figure out, What is the personal space in the Mediterranean? How close can you swim before you can't swim away? Whatever that distance is, France swims inside of it and says, "The water makes me feel so free."

It's not having that effect on me. I've got bear claws to hide and promises to keep. I don't want to keep them, of course, but I don't want to break them with a woman my girlfriend introduced me to, right before returning to our hotel room. This is a liaison too *dangereux.* Plus, the ergonomics of aquatic betrayal are finally hitting me: France may look like a goddess, but like any mortal having sex in the water, she is going to have to stabilize herself, probably by holding my waist. At which point the bear-claw cat will be out of the swimsuit bag. Just the thought of her touching me makes me so tense, I can't breathe normally. Which makes me look . . . abnormal.

France says, "Is everything okay? Maybe we should go?" And she gets up out of the water and stands on the beach, dripping in the moonlight, dabbing at herself with her dress.

That's when it hits me: In my haste to get into the water, I neglected to plan how to get out. I am a man with half a plan! So I've got one eye on France and the other on my shirt, which is hanging on the back of the beach chair. I'm floating closer and closer, as the water gets shallower and shallower, so that only my head is visible, like an alligator. It looks like I'm in about six feet of water, but really it's just a few inches, my hands and feet gingerly scouting the seafloor for sharp rocks, clearing out obstacles to create a smooth launchpad.

Finally, France lifts her dress up over her head.

I am up and out of the water and on that beach, sprinting in my underwear toward the safety of my shirt, like an East German trying to reach Berlin Alexanderplatz before the guards shoot him. In go my arms!

I am wet but covered when France's head pops through her dress hole and she sees me standing right next to her, thirty feet closer than I was a few seconds ago. She stumbles back in surprise, letting out a little French vowel. "O!"

Finally, we get dressed and start walking back through town across the ancient cobblestones, to the hotel at the top of the hill. The cobblestones are a little uneven. So at one point, the backs of our hands brush, and France takes mine in hers. I've read in *Let's Go Europe*—in a "This Means That" cultural translation sidebar—this is often just "a warm and friendly gesture" among European women: "Don't get any ideas." So I'm trying not to get any ideas.

Then France says, "Jane is very lucky to have you." It's a very nice thing to say, if it weren't being said by someone who wished Jane weren't so lucky.

I say, "Thank you. But I'm very lucky to have her, too."

There's a flash in France's otherwise-inscrutable eyes, and I see that my predatory indifference has blinded me to the true vulnerabilities of my prey: France is on vacation with her sister, not her boyfriend. She is beautiful, but she is lonely. "Why?" she says, the smile on her face betrayed by her eyes: What does Jane have that I don't?

I'm as bad at math as I am at philandering: Quantifying the reasons to stay faithful to a profoundly difficult relationship versus sleeping with a French goddess on the beach is way beyond me. So I throw it back at France. "Why are you friends with her?"

France says, "Because she pursued me." To the victor go the spoils.

Our hips bump at the base of the steps leading up to our hotel, and France slides her arm around my waist.

I freeze, like any man trying to avoid the end of life as he knows it. My knees buckle. My torso bends. France's hand slides up my rib cage, lodging in my armpit, as she walks to the step above, trying to maintain contact.

France looks down at me and says, very reasonably, "Shall we walk?"

And we walk. Up. Sending France's hand sliding back down. Until it hits.

France starts laughing her bubbly French laugh. "Softage."

I don't speak French. I'm not learning now. I keep walking.

She says it again, "Softage. You have a . . . how do you say it in English? A life preserver. It's so *cute*." She keeps her hand *right there,* like a girlfriend . . . like someone who cares less about my body than I care about hers!

Up the steps.

Into the lobby.

Into the elevator. It's too small and too bright to be touching in a warm and friendly way. So we stand in opposite corners and just stare at each other while the bell rings for each floor. Would it be wrong to shut off the power and rip off her clothes? (Why else do they put switches in elevators, if not to facilitate dangerous liaisons?)

The doors open, and we step into the hall outside our rooms. France reaches out her hands and takes mine.

I look into her eyes, and see, very clearly, a woman willing to destroy a seven-year relationship for one night of sex: my kind of woman. The problem being, Jane's so deeply a part of me—seven years of me—I can't help seeing France through Jane's eyes. I can't help hearing Jane's voice in my head, saying, You're making a mistake. I lean in and kiss France . . . on the cheek. Three times, like the French, which allows you to change your mind—each kiss comes closer than the last. I squeeze her hands, then let go.

Jane's up in bed, reading *Let's Go Europe,* preparing for the debate we'll be having tomorrow morning at the hydrofoil station.

"How was it?" she says, in her guileless, offhand way.

I say, "Hard. *Really* hard."

Jane looks up and says, "I'm sorry." She knows. She understands why I've been wearing a shirt for a week on a beach vacation, and she accepts it.

I don't. Why can't I have sex with France and a relationship with Jane? Just as Jane has sex with me and a relationship with France? We both want the same things.

I get undressed, get in bed, and turn my back to Jane. Suddenly, I start crying—these weepy little hide-them-in-your-hotel-room-pillow tears—which is not at all the kind of guy I am. But after seven days and seven nights of hiding my body and my thoughts, I am spent . . . and France is gone, and I can't help wishing I'd gone with her. But after seven *years,* Jane's still here, warm in bed, lying next to me, flipping through *Let's Go,* and I'm hoping to God I haven't made a mistake; I'm *really* hoping she's the one.

NINETEEN

The Nutcracker

Birds have two houses
One up north, one down south
One shared with the kids and spouse
One reserved for cooling out
Birds do, why can't I?
—song, year eight

Shortly after we got back from Positano, the letters from France began arriving, and with them the painful suntanned, sunblock-scented, moonlight-in-the-Mediterranean-in-only-her-panties-and-bra memories. Just when I'd start to forget, I would open our mailbox and see a blue onionskin *Par Avion* envelope, some austere French personage staring out at me from the stamp in the corner, a postcard from Gallic hell. It amazed me, really, that Jane continued to let a home wrecker into our home, if only through the mail slot.

Of course, I'd never told her how much I fantasized about France wrecking our home. But I figured Jane's spider sense would tell her, even if I did not. That's what makes a woman a woman—she knows more than you do, especially about you. The fact that Jane continued to fraternize with the enemy . . . I didn't know what it meant: Was Jane supremely confident in her superior attractiveness? Trusting in my fidelity? Stupidly trusting in my fidelity? (After all, even I didn't know whether my fidelity could be trusted.) Or, all her seeming guilelessness notwithstanding, was she more cunning than I was—not to mention than France? Was Jane trying to set me up? Put another hen into the henhouse and see if the fox came out?

It did cross my mind to ask Jane what she was thinking, or to tell her what I was thinking. But that would have required an honest conversation, to reveal what I was thinking, and I didn't want to reveal what I was thinking, because I wanted to keep thinking it. Mushrooms need darkness to thrive. And I liked my mushrooms, even if they were poisonous mushrooms, toxic to my mental health, and to the health of our relationship. I almost had sex with France in the Mediterranean and, just as damning, I *didn't* have sex in the Mediterranean with Jane. Both were painful thoughts to live with. I played with pain, like any man who has been trained to suppress his thoughts and feelings and desires—that is, any man. I figured one day the pain would go away, or—worst case—I would die. Either way, my suffering would end.

Then one day, Jane walked into our living room from the bedroom, holding in one hand an opened blue onionskin envelope with the little red-and-dark-blue airmail border, and in the other a few sheets of blue onionskin paper covered in handwriting.

"Guess what?" said Jane, so completely focused on her own

excitement at having a European friend, she could not see the philandering forest for the platonic trees. "France is coming to New York!"

I sat motionless at the news, like a medicated catatonic, which now I was—overdosed on terror at the prospect of consummating my desire for France, and destroying my relationship with Jane. Overdosed on anger: How could Jane willfully expose me—*us*—to such temptation? Overdosed on joy: Thank goodness Jane would expose me to such temptation! And, most of all, overdosed on longing: There is a point in a monogamous relationship—certainly in mine—when you forget completely the moment you wanted to take your companion's clothes off more than you wanted anything in the world, when every part of your body and brain and *being* wondered what she was like *down there,* when you believed that if only you could get in there, you could leave behind the world, or at least the parts of it that didn't work for you. Time would stop, and you would be where you should be: no more seeking, no more hunting, totally alive, yet free from care—immortal. *Le petit mort.*

Okay, maybe not every man thinks that way. But I did. And so did Paris, the Greek god. Who kidnapped Helen, the Greek goddess. And France, the French goddess, lives in Paris, the City of Light. While I, the mere mortal, live in New York, the city that never sleeps, sleepless, thinking about France, the French goddess, assuming she would be an ocean away from me in France, the country, for the rest of my mortal, monogamous life. Which would eventually end, thank God. Because I did not have the nerve either to kidnap France, the French goddess, from

Paris, the city, the way Paris the god had done to Helen, or to leave Jane, my loyal, beautiful, but Teutonic (and therefore, some might say, barbarian) companion—at least in this lifetime. Which will be repeated, again and again and again, ad infinitum, according to the philosopher Nietzsche, as time is infinite and matter finite and one day, in the endless procession of days, our atoms will eventually pass this way again, reconfigure precisely this way, making us miserable all over again—and again and again—according to the theory of eternal recurrence. That's if one believes Nietzsche, which I did, in college, before I discovered that he discovered this truth after he lost his mind from contracting brain-boring syphilis from a prostitute.

None of which I was about to share with Jane, the woman I shared my life and bed with, and considered my best friend. Because friends don't let friends know about their nefarious sexual longings.

"Isn't that great?" said Jane.

"I guess," I said, cool and still, like a spider looking at a fly about to land on his web. "If you like her."

"You don't like her?"

"She's French." Which was true. "I hate French women." Also true. Neglecting to mention the higher (that is, lower) truth: I love French women when they let me have sex with them.

"If you are having wolf thoughts," said Jane—*wolf* being our friendly argot for "creature willing to violate any promise to satisfy his sexual appetites"—"forget it. France told me you are not her type." As though France, not Jane and—best of all—not me, were responsible for satisfying my sexual appetites. Like I was a boy, not a man.

"'I am happy your relationship with James is going better,'" Jane read from the blue onionskin, like a lawyer. "'He seems like a very nice boy.'"

WAIT A MINUTE!

"'Though I assure you, not the kind of boy I find attractive.'"

THEN WHY DID YOU FLOAT YOUR PROFITEROLES IN THIS BOY'S FACE IN THE MEDITERRANEAN?

"'My relationship with you, Jane, means more to me than any boy.'"

I wanted to tell Jane so badly that France was a lying, duplicitous woman. Which would, of course, expose that I was a lying, duplicitous . . . boy. But just as in war, in the battle for potential illicit sex, the first casualty is the truth.

"She's spending Christmas with a friend in Brooklyn," said Jane as I listened quietly. "Why not let her stay with us for New Year's?"

I scanned our apartment: two tiny rooms in a brownstone walk-up; a tiny bathroom not even soundproofed, right off a tiny galley kitchen; about 450 square feet total; nowhere more than three or four steps from anywhere else—small enough to literally leap into each other's arms from anywhere. "If that's what you want."

France would spend Christmas with her friend in Brooklyn. Jane and I would spend it with our respective families out of town. Then we'd all meet up in Manhattan and ring in the New Year together. That was the plan.

Then a few days before Christmas, France called to say she

had arrived from Paris and her friend in Brooklyn was throwing a party.

Why postpone joy?

France's friend lived in a railroad apartment. We opened the door, walked down a long hallway, toward a table laden with candles, bottles of red wine, and piles of sliced red and green peppers, and continued around the corner. Seated in the living room on what can only be described as a wicker throne, in a black cocktail dress set off by a thick pearl choker, hair up in a French twist with tortoise combs, legs crossed, a glass of red wine in one hand, the other extended on the armrest, looking like a cross between Coco Chanel and the mistress of a Southeast Asian dictator, was France.

I met her eyes from across the room.

She smiled without opening her mouth.

Jane opened hers. "Hi!"

I walked back to the table, as though I'd come for the vegetables.

A few minutes later Jane called out, in all seriousness, "You remember France?"

"Yes," I said, sounding serious, as though recalling a distant memory. "Welcome to New York." I kissed her three times on the cheek, the way the French do. Then I retreated, while Jane and France chatted, and chatted, and chatted. Until the guests had gone, as had the peppers, mostly into my now-nauseated stomach, leaving France, the hostess, and us.

France said her friend was the press agent for *The Nutcracker,* which was being put on at the Brooklyn Academy of Music. "She gave me two tickets for tomorrow's performance," said

France. "Can I invite you to join me, Jane?" (France's slightly formal English-as-a-second-language locution being another of her charms.)

Jane said, "I am flying out tomorrow to be with my family. Remember?"

"Oh, yes," said France. "I forgot."

"But James isn't going till the day after tomorrow," said Jane.

France looked me square in the eyes but with a slightly veiled look, like a peregrine falcon behind the translucent nictitating membranes she drops down to shield her eyes from wind and blood and bone as she dives into her prey. "Can I invite you?"

I'm sitting at the Brooklyn Academy of Music next to France, sharing an armrest, brushing her bare arm with my suit jacket, wondering how close is too close.

It's a long two and a half hours staying just over the halfway mark of the armrest. Finally, the show ends and the lights rise and France takes my hand in hers. Hmmm. This may have seemed harmless in Europe, where I guess it's normal to touch each other for reasons other than suggesting or having sex. But when you touch an American guy in America who's been touching the same woman for eight years, and your name is France, you're telling him, this feels *good*. At least, that's what I'm hearing, and who's the American here? She says, "What do we do now?"

"Are you hungry?" I ask, The best way to suppress one appetite being to satisfy another.

France says, "Very."

Up we stand, and down the aisle we go toward the exit, baby-stepping our way out of the theater with the rest of the holiday crowd, jostling into each other's curves and bumps. Offering a spatial preview, a line of physical Braille that reads, "I am an awesome French goddess," and, in my case, "My life preserver feels so much better resting atop a pair of pants versus a swimsuit." Through the lobby, to the sidewalk . . . to the entrance of the subway . . . down the stairs to the train to Manhattan . . . up the stairs and down the street to the Time Café, on the corner of Lafayette.

Plenty of free tables at this hour, surprisingly. Evidently, a late bite at a sleek nightspot is not so hot at Christmastime. We are seated right away, and quickly served a round of drinks. I sit in my chair, facing France on the banquette, like it's any other night with anybody else, feigning interest in everything but France: the bread basket, the clock on the wall, whose hands move in reverse, and—once dinner is served—the food, shoveling it in at a steady rate that balances decorum with terror, like a morphine drip, satiating all of my drives *except* curiosity. "I never understood what you and Jane see in each other," I say. "You're so . . . *different.*"

It's a roundabout way of asking, Why do I want to have sex with you so badly, given how utterly unlike my girlfriend you are?

France says, "She pursued me." As she told me in Positano.

Now I see that France and I share the Rosetta stone of attraction. Jane was aggressive. Jane *is* aggressive. Which makes me feel like a woman.

France makes me feel like a man.

Because she acts like a woman.

Except . . . didn't *she* suggest we do something after *The Nut-cracker*?

Didn't *she* invite me to *The Nutcracker* to begin with?

Didn't *she* say when we went swimming in the Mediterra-nean, alone, at night, in our underwear, that the water made her feel free?

Who's chasing whom?

Who am I kidding? She's chasing me, while making me think I'm chasing her. The French know how to do that kind of thing. I don't have the guts to even introduce myself to a French god-dess, much less pursue one, any more than I have the guts to betray my girlfriend. But none of that really matters, does it? Whether France is aggressive or passive is not the reason I am sitting here well past midnight at the Time Café, eating salmon filet roasted in black sesame seeds. I am sitting at the Time Café because France is beautiful (it was not breasts that launched a thousand ships); and she is new—they call them novelty stores in Times Square for a reason—and most of all, she is sitting here with me at the Time Café, eating salmon filet roasted in black sesame seeds, too. She made herself *available*.

And there is no crime of the heart, or of any other part of the body, so easily justified to one's better self (and, after one's worse self is discovered, one's better half) as a crime of opportu-nity. Let's say you can't pay your rent and you find a wallet full of twenties on the subway. Are you really going to leave it there? Far more valuable than money, the scarcest treasure in all of God's creation, is a beautiful woman willing to share her beauty. If you stumble across an offer like that, it's against nature to return it, or at least against a man's nature, or maybe just against my nature. What am I supposed to do if she offers herself to me? Say no? It'd be an insult to God to say no. Am I willing to insult God and beauty for the sake of truth? No, I am not!

The lights go up, I look up, and France and I are the only people sitting in the Time Café. The busboys, bartender, waiters, and manager are standing there, eyeing our coffee cups and table linens like ravens circling roadkill. It's two o'clock in the morning, according to the clock that runs backward on the wall of the Time Café. Well past bedtime. Especially since I have a plane to catch in the morning, back home for the holidays.

"What should we do now?" says France. It's the same question she asked after *The Nutcracker*, her siren song.

"Would you like an after-dinner drink?" I say without irony. Philandering and sequential logic are not strange bedfellows: We just had dinner. It's after. Let's drink. And after that let's . . .

"Yes," says France. "I would."

We walk down the street to the Temple Bar and have after-dinner drinks.

When they turn up the lights at 4:00 A.M., France and I are once again the only people in the room not on the company payroll.

"Breakfast?" I say, again without irony. Just as day follows night, so does breakfast follow after-dinner drinks—granted, usually with an intervening sleep, and a workday between them. But consistency is the hobgoblin of little monogamous minds.

One cab ride later, France and I are facing each other in a booth at the Empire Diner, which never closes, customers stumbling in from places that do close: club kids, C students, hookers, transvestites, transvestite hookers, philanderers. These are my people.

"Do they have French toast in France?" I ask France, looking at the laminated menu for something that will satisfy the minimum order without making me hurl, suppressing my desire to know her body with my desire to know an inane fact. Which is why I am much better at Trivial Pursuit than I am at the pursuit of women.

"*French* toast?" says France, confused by my taste in games as much as I am confused by hers.

A few minutes later—the Empire being a model of efficiency—I am cutting into my second meal in as many hours, chased by my third (or fourth, or fifth?) drink. I'm nauseated, intoxicated, exhausted . . . but still fixated on the shadows in France's cleavage. They're disappearing. Opportunity is vanishing. Light streaks the sky. It's the moment all vampires and would-be philanderers fear, but one ambivalent philanderers welcome. I am running out of time to cheat. Thank God.

France says, "I've always wanted to see the sunrise in Manhattan. Do you know a roof?" Confirming that it's hard sometime to tell God from the Devil.

I know a roof. It would be lying to tell her I don't. Am I a liar? Besides, what can happen on a tar beach in winter that didn't happen on a sand beach in summer? Plus, it is just the friendly thing to do. And I am nothing if not friendly.

We catch a cab downtown to my office in SoHo. France stands on the sidewalk, soaking up what's left of the night, as I walk in to the twenty-four-hour deli next door to my office building to buy a bottle of water.

"Anything else?" asks the clerk, a condom rack behind his head, rows of colorful, happy-looking little boxes, with writing that jumps out at you: "Like Wearing Nothing at All" . . . "Maximum Endurance" . . . "For *Her* Pleasure."

I want to say, One of those. But we're just here to see the sunrise. "No," I say, perhaps the saddest "No" ever spoken in this deli.

I lead France through the lobby, into the elevator, then press the button for the top floor. We stand in opposite corners, as we did in our hotel in Positano. Only this time, France's sister is in another country. My girlfriend is in another state. We are alone.

The elevator opens, we step through a fire door, and we're back outside, standing on black tar, France in front of me, surrounded by a green oxidized cornice, looking up at the sky through the iron struts and giant tank of a water tower, both of us facing east as the sun rises.

France turns and says, "This is so beautiful."

I say, "Yes, it is," and I kiss her—the first *other* woman I've kissed in four thousand sunrises. Four presidential administrations. A *long* time. I kiss her again, and again.

France whispers, "Do you have a condom?"

What did I think was going to happen up here? That we were going to look at the sunrise? In December?

"No," I say, furious at having walked past the condom rack out of loyalty to Jane. I knew this might happen. I knew what I was doing. But proud at having walked past the condom rack out of loyalty to Jane. This is the price of monogamy: profoundly upsetting, soul-searing sexual frustration. *Exactly* why I don't want to be monogamous!

France smiles her wicked Mona Lisa smile—somehow animating her face without opening her mouth, revealing appetite while concealing the means of satisfying it. It's an amazing feat of physiognomy, which maybe all Latinate women can perform. Perhaps because Latinate languages, such as French, emphasize vowels over consonants. When you've said *oui* thousands of times as a French girl, your cheeks flower in a way that allows you to say yes by the time you are a French woman, without moving a muscle. And at sunrise on a roof in the middle of Manhattan with two meals and five drinks and no sleep inside of me, it's awesome.

I smile back at France, but I suspect my bared teeth make me look more like an American wolf than a portrait by an old master.

Then I look at my watch, punctuality—loyalty to time—an easier mark to hit than loyalty to people, and one of the few redeeming signs of a dependable character in an otherwise unreliable partner. "My flight!"

We rush downstairs.

I put France in a cab to Brooklyn.

Catch another cab home to pack—nauseated, intoxicated, sleep-deprived, humiliated. What will I say to Jane? Nothing! It's my perfume-scented cross to bear. Still, how could I have traded seven years of fidelity for a few minutes with those irresistible French lips? Easily! Even though I can see now in the literal light of day that I could have and should have resisted. Sometimes, even I am in awe of how bad my judgment is.

When I open my front door, I see right away that my life is going to get worse. Our bed is unmade. My answering machine is blinking the number 24 in red, meaning twenty-four new messages have come in since I left last night for *The Nutcracker.*

The first is from Jane: "Hi, honey, my flight was canceled." Due to weather. "They put me on another plane in the morning. See you soon."

That's why the bed is unmade!

The next eight or nine messages are also from Jane, all recorded from *inside* the apartment (where Jane slept last night, alone) using the memo button, all of them essentially the same, varying only the time of day:

"It's one . . ."

"It's two . . ."

"It's three . . .

"It's four in the morning . . ."

Followed by, "Where *are* you? Oh my God!"

And the next dozen are also from Jane, all recorded from outside the apartment, starting at La Guardia Airport and ending at the St. Louis Airport, where her new flight was grounded en route, due to weather. "I trusted you," she says. "You bastard!"

Not withstanding I haven't slept in a day, I am suddenly wide awake.

I pack.

Race to the airport.

Barely make my plane.

Once we've reached cruising altitude and the in-flight services begin, I start calling directory assistance from my seat, using Airfone, to get the numbers of all the hotels around the

St. Louis Airport. It's ten bucks a call, so it costs me about $170 to get from the Best Western Motel to the Roadway Inn, then another $70 to find the hotel Jane's checked herself into, and then another $100 on top of that before she'll stop hanging up on me long enough to hear me plead, soto voce (to shield the demise of my relationship from the passenger next to me), "I swear to God, I did not have sex with that woman!!!" (I was ahead of President Clinton by ten years.)

"How can you spend all night with someone and not have sex?"

"It wasn't easy," I say. "Which doesn't mean I didn't want to."

"What does that mean?"

"We've been together seven years," I tell her, before whispering, "and I want to know what another woman is like. And I don't know what to do. Unlike France, who wants to fly out to be with me, by the way. Would that be all right, honey—just to work through my feelings?"

"What?" says Jane. "Are you crazy? Is she crazy?"

"She's your friend."

"I'm going to call her right now," says Jane. "I'm going to meet her when I get back to New York. I'm going to look her in the eye and ask her, 'Why are you doing this to me?' Merry Christmas, James." *Click.*

A few days later—after a very unmerry Christmas with my family—I'm back in New York in our apartment, taking a shower, when Jane comes home from the airport. Looking through the crack in the shower curtain, I can see she's wearing a beautiful blue cashmere cape. She looks fabulous, which is evidently how a woman looks after you've betrayed her, when you finally have to face she can get along without you.

Jane says, "Hi."

I get out of the shower.

We have the best sex ever: postbetrayal sex. I had no idea Jane could do these things.

"How could you even think of leaving me?" she says.

"I'm a man?"

"A *man* makes choices," says Jane. "I'm going to lunch with France."

A few hours later, Jane comes back and reports what happened. "France broke down sobbing," she says. "And begged me for forgiveness. I read her the letter she sent me, out loud, about how our friendship was more important than any man. She said that was before she got to me know me, and that I didn't deserve you, and that she was going to steal you away."

I say, *"Really?"* Not that I wait to be stolen away, but it's nice to have options, and is a small harem really out of the question?

"You may feel flattered," says Jane. "But I feel sorry for France. Any woman who would destroy a friendship with me for a blow job with you . . ."

Blow job? Maybe France wants to make Jane jealous. Or maybe France feels as embarrassed as I do—as long as she's going to lose her friendship with Jane, she might as well lose it for a legitimate sex act listed in the *Kama Sutra*. Or maybe—just maybe—Jane is bluffing.

Whatever the explanation, I don't correct her. If Jane's all right with my getting a blow job from France, maybe I *can* get one! If I'm gonna do the time, I'm gonna do the crime.

"I would never do that to a friend," says Jane. "I'm so much stronger than she is. If you want her, you can have her. But you're making a mistake."

The next night, I meet France at a café, to see for myself.

She's sitting at a corner table, candlelight flickering across her glorious face, as I sit down on the opposite side.

France tells me about her meeting with Jane, how upsetting it was, but how—upon reflection—Jane didn't deserve me. How she, France, does—like she is satisfying the natural order by using her feminine gifts to cater to my masculine drive, which Jane doesn't understand.

I hold France's hand and start sucking on her fingers like a man, or a masculine animal, anyway.

France looks at me with stars in her eyes—reflected light from the candles, granted, but still. She *is* a goddess, but the power of a goddess is reflected by the man who worships her. France sees her power in me. "Whatever happens," she says, "let us make love . . . one time."

I look at France's dress. It's the same dress she wore to *The Nutcracker*: black, which is good, but full of holes that have been ripped on purpose, then pinned with safety pins; it's a cross between a dress and a bandage. I guess this is high fashion. But I can't take it seriously. I can't take her seriously. I can't take us seriously.

I suck on her fingers one more time—to remember. Because this may be the last other woman I ever taste. Then I put down her hand and say, "I can't. I can't begin a relationship like this, and I can't end one like this. I'm sorry."

France walks out, leaving me alone with the taste of her little French fingers.

A few apology-filled days and nights later, Jane and I are at home taking a bath. Jane's in front, I'm behind, and we're talking about the New Year, the old year, us.

I say, "You should never have invited France to visit."

Jane says, "You could have told me you didn't want her here."

"But I did want her here," I say. "It's your job to keep her away."

"Don't blame me because you couldn't control yourself," says Jane. "I don't want to be your jailer."

I like the sound of *that.* I really do. Vows of fidelity are noble aspirations, and I, for one, happen to believe in them. But how can a man in his late twenties possibly forsake all others when there is so much testosterone inside of him that he can eat and drink ten thousand calories in three sittings over three hours and still not be satiated? "Will you marry me?"

"If you're going to do this again, tell me now."

"I don't know," I say. "I live in doubt and fear and constant confusion." (Which, of course, comes as no surprise to Jane.) "But I am sure I love you." (Which is true.) "Will you marry me?"

"I'll think about it," she says. "I'll think about it."

She turns her head and smiles.

TWENTY

Wedding Invitation

I hope you two have learned the secret of getting along.
Alternate who wins the arguments. Take turns.
—a graduate student in Jane's seminary, after
overhearing us in her room

There's going to be a wedding.

In room 202 of the Houston Hospice.

Tonight.

It's a perfect storybook ending to Kate's Book-of-the-Month Club life. After forty-some years of reading books (Kate was a precocious reader) written by women, for women, about women who are attracted to men who aren't suited to those women— either because of the men's natures (shiftless or restless) or their occupations (none or all-consuming)—Kate is going to marry a restless man without an occupation . . . again! (Unless you consider it an occupation to try not to have a nervous breakdown or become violently unhinged while defending yourself against legal threats from your dying fiancée's unhinged family. But really, is this the time or the place for a nuanced appreciation of character?)

The only problem is, Kate is not on the same page as the rest of the family. She's reading a romance. They're reading true crime, which is what they usually read. Only instead of this being a story about one family member plotting against another, this time the danger is from *outside*: There's only one thing a twenty-nine-year-old rock drummer without a rock band and with hair to his waist could possibly want from a bald, forty-eight-year-old, postmastectomy, terminally ill woman who is wasting away in a nightgown on her deathbed: to steal her money!

I've pointed out to my family the "You'd think it was so obvious, you wouldn't need to point it out" fact that Kate has no money. She doesn't even have health insurance. If and when she dies, all she'll leave Roger is memories and debt. And regardless of any secret venal motivations he may have, who else would want to be with a bald, forty-eight-year-old, postmastectomy, terminally ill woman on her deathbed? Some people might call him a saint! I think she's lucky to have him.

This all makes sense to my family, in a "When you put it like that, I can see your point" way, inspiring them to temporarily bottle their rage with reason. Then the mind-altering grief of losing a daughter or sister destroys reason and everything else, except sorrow—if you're lucky. If you're not, all that's left is blind fury. It's like yeast in otherwise-bitter fruit: What little sweetness there was gets metabolized, transforming deeply unhappy women and men into 100-proof rageaholics.

And that's *before* they find out they're going to a wedding tonight. If I tell them Kate and Roger are engaged, they'll go berserk. Someone may actually get hurt—on top of the psychic wounds they'll inflict upon one another, and then on Kate. Why should a family with no boundaries start building them now?

I want Kate's last days filled with peace and love, which was exactly what I told the social worker when we checked Kate into the hospice.

"That's a nice idea," said the social worker, forcing a weak smile, truly pained by my naïveté. "That's a noble idea. Really. But in my experience, people usually die the way they lived. Maybe it's not your job to make things right." In other words, you can't protect people from themselves.

And if you can't protect people from themselves, they can't protect you. You are on your own.

Who wants to admit *that*?

TWENTY-ONE

When Someone Hits the Nail on the Head, It Hurts

You're right, we are engaged—in warfare!
—to Jane, year eight

After we stopped seeing Jackie, the therapist who suggested that Jane have me incarcerated, we began planning our wedding, and seeing Elke, the European sex therapist who postulated that we weren't copulating enough—at least at the same time, with each other—and were replacing copulating with bickering.

Tall, handsome, and lanky, like a man, Elke had a deep, velvety baritone, which, in the service of that elegant accent of indeterminate geographic origin, and a mien that mixed the prurient with the academic, projected the conflicted aura of European porn packaged as an art-house film, or a dominatrix with a Ph.D. (Which she may have been. There were dozens of books on her shelves with *Power* and/or *Sex* on the spines.) Elke was someone who either by training or inclination could sit next to you on a bed, taking notes as you copulated. Which *could* have been cool; I'm as perverted as the next guy, or transgendered gal. But, quite frankly, Elke just wasn't hot enough to go down that dark road with us. And something about the look in her eyes reminded me of my own. And one sexually frustrated masculine type in the bedroom was already one too many.

It was at this sexless fork in the road that Jane and I agreed that we needed to suspend our interviews with possibly transgendered sex therapists (When *they're* confused about whether they're a man or a woman, can they help you be a woman or a man?), stop bargain-hunting for trainees (Does anyone genuinely competent take patient calls at midnight on a Friday?), and find a serious, expensive *professional.* Someone who made more money than we did. Who was smarter than we were. With a Ph.D. *and* an academic affiliation in lieu of a license. (Unlike licensed therapists treating troubled individuals, in New York State, a therapist needs absolutely no credentials to be a couples counselor, that is to treat two deeply troubled individuals, as long as she treats them at the same time, the thinking being, The greater the psychological problems, the less training one needs to treat them.) We needed someone like Marilyn, the head of marital counselor training at NYU.

Right away, I could see Marilyn was a peer, and then some: She inhabited a refined but humane office furnished in wood and fabric (which at this level of refinement must be called upholstery) on Central Park West; and she wore a suit that hung somewhere on the sartorial spectrum between Chanel and Brooks Brothers—feminine, but indicating she was here to solve problems, not have sex. She began our session by asking us to state our issues in a few minutes. When we had finished, Marilyn asked me, "Have you apologized for your behavior?"

I said, "The part that's true, yes."

Marilyn turned to Jane. "Have you apologized for your behavior?"

Jane said, "It's not my fault."

Marilyn turned to me and said, "Does she ever take responsibility for *anything*?"

Yes! proclaimed the invisible bubble caption that opened over my head. Revenge is a dish best served discreetly, I have learned over the contentious years, either by a patient advocate or a trained mental-health professional acting as your messenger from Sanity Land, allowing you to prevail in your battle of the sexes without seeming to take up arms—no fingerprints on that brickbat. Unfortunately, such victories are also short-lived, as the queen of the castle, when faced with bad news, generally shoots the messenger.

Fifty minutes later, I was standing on the sidewalk on Central Park West, listening to Jane tell me what she wanted in our *next* therapist. Jane said that Marilyn's style of therapy was known as "confrontational."

"We need someone nurturing." Like the parents we never had, who never had those parents, either.

Which meant that now we were looking for someone who did not exist, had never existed, and never would exist, which—when you are an extraordinarily persistent person, as Jane was, or an extraordinarily obsessively compulsive person, as I was—could keep you searching for a while.

TWENTY-TWO

The Night I Beat My Inner Loser

I'm tired of wandering
I'm tired of home
I'm tired of everything
Leave me alone
Too tired to move
Too scared to stop
Blocked
—song, year twelve

This is a bad night at Max Fish. I'm feeling bad about myself and my wife and our not-enough-sex life, and I'm feeling really bad about my wife's brother, Huey, and his sex life. It's getting better right in front of me. He's just moved up from Charleston, South Carolina, and we're in a booth at the back of the bar, having "Welcome to New York" drinks with a couple of friends. One of them, Sophia, this stunning Italian woman in a microskirt, thinks he's funny. She's actually laughing at his jokes. And he's guf-FAWing away, in his up-from-Charleston, ten-decibels-too-loud, tremendously irritating hayseed way. And the whole gang's laughing and guffawing with them, and congratulating Huey for his supposed achievements.

"How'd you find an apartment for five hundred dollars a *month* off *Central Park West?*"

"How'd you get that gig at the film studio?"

And when Sophia goes to the bathroom, one of them asks, "Where'd you meet *her?*"

The answer to all these questions is: *Me!* He's subletting *my* studio, got a job through *my* wife, met Sophia through *my* friends. But Huey doesn't say a word. He just sits there with this strong-but-silent-type look on his face. Like he's actually *done* something beyond using my connections. Like *he's the alpha male.*

I'm the alpha male! *I* deserve the attention. *I* deserve Sophia. But there's no way to prove it. I'm married, and my wife's sitting next to me. All I can do is sit and stew, with Huey guffawing away, and make believe I'm happy for him.

There's a pool table at Max Fish, and after getting my fill of phony toasts, I walk over to shoot off some steam. The reigning champion is the off-duty bartender, a soft-spoken Japanese guy who plays every night after work. He's the lord of the table; nobody beats him. But he makes it fun to try. He gives you tips on shot selection, to make it fun for *him*: the cat giving the mouse escape lessons. There are three or four guys ahead of me waiting to challenge him. So I sign my name on the chalkboard and get in line. And three or four games later, it's me versus the lord, and I lose. Which is exactly how it should be. He's the better player. He deserves to win.

And I start to feel good again. Like there really is a natural order. Like good wins and bad loses and what's happening between Huey and Sophia is just a freak of nature, a When Alpha Things Happen to Beta Males moment that God lets happen sometimes, just to keep you guessing. It's so calming to be reassured that the system works, regardless of the fact that you may be on the losing end.

Then the Shark walks in. He's about five seven, wearing tight black jeans, and is ten or twenty pounds too skinny. I don't know if it's drugs or a fast metabolism, but he's a little pool cue of a guy. He has this *Frampton Comes Alive!* shag that covers everything but a tiny white block of face, only his hair's black instead of blond. Fresh white tuxedo shirt—no collar, like a priest—buttoned all the way up, without a crease. This is 10:30 or 11:00 P.M., and he has a starched shirt on, just to play pool. And the reason you know this is, he's got his own cue—a traveling stick: three sections, polished rosewood, brass fittings. He's screwing it together at the table. The guy has come to win.

He writes his name on the chalkboard. Three or four games later, he's playing the Japanese bartender. Seven shots after that, he's down to the eight ball—in the time it took me to get a beer. He's orders of magnitude better than the bartender, who's orders of magnitude better than everybody else.

So I start to erase my name from the chalkboard. It won't be any fun to lose to this guy. Because he's not playing for fun. He's playing for self-esteem. And I don't have any to spare.

The bartender sees me with the eraser and says, "Don't do that. It's just a game. The worst that can happen is you lose." Now he's just been creamed, and you can see a little shame on his face when he says this, which is perfectly normal under the circumstances. But maybe he just wants me to play so he looks better by comparison? That's what I'd do. But he has this from-a-stable-home vibe, and the Japanese rock-garden thing that makes you feel the world is bigger than a pool game, and that it'll be okay if you lose and you really shouldn't quit.

So I write my name back up. And three or four games later, I'm playing the Shark. I'm the challenger, so I rack the balls. The Shark breaks. And he scratches—shoots too hard and a ball flies off.

And it's my turn. I start sizing up the one shot I'm going to sink. I look at the balls all spread out in front of me, and that's when I see . . . the vision: a schematic diagram of how to run the table; the vectors between the cue ball and the pool balls; the pockets they'll drop into; little circular hash marks where the cue ball will stop after each shot, setting me up for the next shot. Shot by shot by shot, a blueprint for beating the Shark. I'm sure of it.

I have no right to beat this guy. I never play. I have no real skill. I just got lucky. *He's* the Shark. *He's* the alpha. He *deserves* to win. And what's more, he *needs* to win. He's got a starched white shirt and his own pool cue; this is his *life*. I should throw this game, so he can feel good about himself. It's my job to protect his self-esteem. Just as he would protect mine if he got lucky.

Those are the voices at war in my head: You can win. You should lose. And I don't know which to listen to.

I start making shots, six in a row. I'm down to one ball plus the eight ball in minutes. It's incredible. I've never played this well in my life. And everyone feels the tension. The losers are gathered around the table like the gallery at a golf match. The Shark's sitting down, peeling labels off of beer bottles. I'm trying to stop my elbow from twitching. I'm realizing, for the first time in my life, that I *like* losing, or at least I understand it. It's what I know. I'm the kid everybody consoles: "Sorry you lost, but hang in there and one day when you grow up, you'll win." And I don't want to grow up. I like being a kid.

I twitch and shoot and miss.

The Shark's on his feet. *Boom-boom-boom,* he starts dropping balls in, just like he did to the bartender. Then he misses—an incredibly easy shot. And I get a second chance.

I sink the next shot and I'm down to the eight ball; one more ball to go. Make it and win, or miss it and lose. Those are the choices. He won't screw up again.

I can barely breathe, I'm so tense.

And the Shark's distressed to the point of trying pool voodoo. He walks over to the opposite side of the table, sits down, and looks at me looking at the eight ball. His head is just above the pocket. When I lean over to size up my shot, I see the eight ball in the middle, and on either side, his eyes; one, two, three little orbs in a row, two of them with pupils. He looks so pathetic, with his "The only thing I have in life to feel good about is pool, so don't take it away from me" expression, which makes me think it'll kill him if I win. And it'll kill me, too—the loser in me. And I want to miss the shot *so* badly and go back to the booth and have the "Better luck next time; keep trying" pep talk I've been having my whole life. I want . . . the attention.

But one of the voices says, See how it feels to win. Just once.

So I take a deep breath. Freeze my elbow. Strike the cue ball. Sink the eight.

High fives all around. "Incredible shooting, man!" "Wow, I never seen anything like that!"

The Shark's slumped in his chair, surrounded by empties with the labels peeled off. It's like a ticker-tape parade on the floor around him.

I walk over and shake his hand. Tell him, "Good game." Lose the next game.

Then I go back to the booth. Everybody's still welcoming Huey to New York. Jane turns to me and says, "What happened?"

I say, "I just beat the best pool player I've ever seen."

Jane says, "That's great!" And she rejoins the "Welcome to New York, Huey" party.

I'm alone in my own limelight. A psychological revolution has occurred. The dominant part of my personality, the Inner Loser, has been overthrown; the tiny little Inner Winner has triumphed. The world is a completely different place for me at this moment, and nobody cares—not least, my wife.

This is what it means to get what you want in life. When you reach the top of the mountain, you're alone. And there's no need for anyone below to say you'll make it next time. Because you've already made it. Your membership in the Losers' Club, all that camaraderie, it's over. You're on your own. It's an incredibly lonely feeling. So I start to pray: Please, God, do me a favor. Please make Huey feel this way when he wakes up tomorrow morning with Sophia and please help me wake up thinking of Jane.

TWENTY-THREE

A Medically Necessary Miniskirt

I can't help shake the feeling that I missed out on something important by not dating. I overheard two women at a bar on 77ᵗʰ talking to each other about e-mail. I said, "Excuse me, you have e-mail?" One said, "What do you mean?" I said, "My wife told me most women don't have e-mail. That it's a guy thing. That any woman who has e-mail is trying to be a guy." They looked at me like I was crazy. The bartender said, "You poor dude." Then he asked me if I wanted another margarita.
—journal entry

I hadn't had sex for about a year, because (a) I was married, (b) sleeping with my wife reminded me of the hundreds of women I imagined I would otherwise have slept with had I never married her seven years ago, on top of the eight years we were together before that, stirring up deep and painful feelings of my unrealized inner Casanova, and yet (c) I was monogamous.

Therefore, (d) I was spending a lot of time alone, trying not to think about having sex. Which meant avoiding anything that made me think about people: friends, neighbors, movies, magazines, books, looking out my window. I lived in solitary confinement for a year, except for trips to coffee shops and pizza parlors, trying not to notice the other customers.

But one idle evening I break down and walk to my neighborhood bookstore, where I open up *The Group,* by Mary McCarthy, and start reading. I thought it was literature, a story about somebody else's life that would make me forget my own. But when I get to page 36, I find myself reading about the life I'd been trying not to think about: A charismatic bum who lives downtown opens his door, to find a young virgin who's just graduated from Vassar and moved to New York, and who desperately wants the bum to take her virginity as a kind of graduation present. So for the next five pages, in graphic detail, they have a carnal commencement.

I buy the book, and reread that scene in the comfort and privacy of my own home, which sets me to thinking: Why can't my life be like that? *I'm* a charismatic bum. Why isn't Jane a virgin from Vassar? Why am I living *my* life when I could be living his?

A few days later, Jane and I are sitting on a bench in Central Park next to the bronze of Alice in Wonderland, having one of our "What women really want" arguments—the old sex versus love debate, which I invariably lose, getting neither sex nor love as a consolation prize—when I bring up *The Group* as proof that, deep down, what women really want is casual sex. Not that I'd had any. But I *could* have had some, I tell her, had we not married so young. *I coulda been a sexual contender.* I know what women want, according to no less an authority than Mary McCarthy, who, in addition to being a novelist specializing in women, is first and foremost a woman herself.

Jane looks at me like I'm nuts—which I am, because I haven't had sex in a year. I'm in love with a woman with whom I can't avoid conflict, but I am also passionately conflict averse. The only way to hide from fighting is to hide from every kind of intimacy. I don't know that we ever had make-up sex, apart from the France debacle. But when you've gotten in as many arguments as we have, make-up sex would be tantamount to nymphomania. Sadly, *that* disorder has yet to visit this marriage. Jane says, "All the women in *The Group* kill themselves."

"You're telling me the *ending*?"

"Well, maybe not all," says Jane. "But some."

"You've ruined the book!" I scream at her, sitting in the shadow of the Mad Hatter.

"It's so predictable," says Jane with the icy confidence of a Smith graduate, so unlike the heated desperation of the ingenue from Vassar. "Any woman who has casual sex has low self-esteem. You should have seen that coming."

"What are you, God?"

"No," says Jane. "I'm a woman."

It's how these arguments always end.

That's why our arguments always drive me crazy. Because I'm not getting any sex, and I didn't get *much* before I stopped getting *any,* so I don't have much experience to fight back with. I can never say, with any authority, "You're wrong. *Normal* women are really like this." Because I don't know any normal women. I know Jane, and before her, I knew Anna, who became a paranoid schizophrenic shortly after she dumped me for art school and I wrote "The Devils You Know." I've been on two first dates *in my life*—one of them with a woman who was clinically insane, and the other with a woman who is driving me crazy.

I go to a clinical psychologist to talk about it, suggested by my health insurance company, he's conveniently located in the neighborhood just a few blocks up from Marilin the confrontational marriage counselor.

"All I can think about is having sex," I tell him a few moments after sitting down in his office for the first time.

"That's perfectly normal," he says.

"With someone other than my wife."

"Ah."

"We've been together fifteen years," I say. "I've been looking at the same two breasts for four presidential administrations. I want to see a new pair."

My psychologist scratches his pseudo-Freudian close-cropped salt-and-pepper beard and says, "What do you want me to do?"

"Help me stop wanting to cheat."

He gives me a vaguely smug 'If it were that easy to solve people's problems, I wouldn't be solving yours' smile. "It doesn't work that way," he says. "You have to make a commitment first—to cheat or to not cheat. Then act on your decision. *Then* I can help you deal with the consequences."

"I don't want consequences," I say. The searing agony of divorce, the bitter self-loathing of duplicity, or the unendurable pain of fidelity are the only paths I can see at the moment. Who would commit to any of those? "I want to change the way I *feel*."

"I'm a big believer in taking action," says my psychologist. "Let me ask you a question: What's keeping you from having sex with another woman?"

"My wife."

"Really? It's a moral issue?"

"Even if I weren't married," I say, taking his bait, "we've been together so long, I don't know how to meet women anymore."

"Now we have something to work with," says my psychologist. "Take off your watch and ask for the time."

"You're not serious?"

"I tell that to all my male patients. I'm not here to judge what's right or wrong," he says. "My job is help you get what you want in life. And if you want to meet women, ask enough of them the time and you'll meet one who likes you. It's a numbers game. You have to decide whether to play it."

"What woman worth sleeping with would have an adulterous affair with a total stranger who doesn't even know what time it is?"

"Take off your watch and find out."

The anthropologist in me was aroused: Who would be left inside of a behavioral filter designed by a clinical psychologist to separate out from the general population women who are attracted to an incompetent, philandering, sexually deprived, depraved, and altogether-desperate male—that is, the real me?

On the other hand, do I really want to know who is really

attracted to the real me? Do *I* want to know the real me? This is precisely why the notion of actually changing your life instead of just talking about changing it is dangerously glamorized. Why take painful action to change your life when you can sustain it forever by talking about how miserable you are? It's the difference between being human and being immortal. Who wants to be human?

"Thanks for the tips," I say. "I'd prefer to talk things through." I tell him that I met Jane when I was twenty-two and she was twenty-five and I was about to drop out of college and she was on a scholarship and I saw that to keep her, to defend my territory against the advances of male scholarship students, I'd have to perform at a higher level. So I started getting straight A's and moved into her dorm room. Result: I never got to experience the years of shallow, empty, awesome sexual liaisons that are the foundation of every man's sexual self-esteem.

Then at our tenth session—the last session my health insurance company will reimburse me for, unless my psychologist suggests they should pony up for more—the psychologist says, "If you want to keep seeing me, you'll have to pay for it yourself. I'm sorry, but your therapy is not medically necessary."

"'Medically necessary'?"

"Not a mental-health problem," says my psychologist. "It's a *personal* problem. And that's not covered."

"'*Personal*'? I can barely function," I say. "I haven't had sex in a year. *That's* seriously fucked-up. How much more miserable do I have to be to qualify for insurance?"

He ticks off a list of the covered mental-health problems:

"Obsessive-compulsive disorder; substance abuse; clinical depression; suicidal thinking; nymphomania."

That sounds like good news to me. "I either have, have had, or want to have all of those conditions! *Especially* nymphomania," I say. "I just don't have the guts. But I definitely have OCD. I can't eat dessert until I peel the wax off the dinner candles."

"Do you spend five hours a day washing your hands?" he asks.

"This is so depressing."

"Are you so depressed that you can't get out of bed?"

"Sometimes."

"Well, here you are," he says.

"I didn't want to bring this up," I say, laying down my personality disorder trump card, "but I've thought about killing myself. I really have."

"I believe you," says my psychologist. "Have you thought about how you'd do it?"

"Not exactly. It's just a vague desire to disappear."

"I have patients who go to sleep with guns under their pillows," he says. "If you find yourself in that situation, it's reimbursable."

I'm the emotional equivalent of the working poor: distressed, but not distressed enough to qualify for help. It's enough to make me want to put a gun under my pillow.

There's an old adage in New York, and perhaps wherever there are forty-five-minute hours: You get the shrink you deserve. I deserve more than this. At the least, I deserve to be reimbursed for the cost of talking to a trained mental-health professional about my sexual frustrations. Until I neutralize the danger, I will live them out and destroy my marriage. I deserve the talking cure!

What if my psychologist is right? What if I'm incurable? What if you can't talk away your feelings? That you actually have to do something to improve your life?

Then it hits me: If I work on my problem under clinical supervision—in other words, find a gorgeous female mental-health professional who will have sex with me on her couch, decoding the reasons for and thereby neutralizing the danger of such a liaison happening *out there,* in the real world—it wouldn't be cheating. It would be therapy!

I call up my health insurance company and I tell them my psychologist misdiagnosed me and that I want another introductory ten-pack of covered sessions with another psychologist, someone who will give me a second opinion. "She just has to be a woman," I say. "On the Upper West Side." Gender and convenience are no less important in a therapeutic sexual liaison than they are in a conventional relationship.

They give me a few names and numbers.

I call them all. Like any man choosing a woman on the basis of an outgoing message on a telephone answering machine, I make an appointment with the woman with the sexiest voice.

At our first meeting, at the appointed time, the door opens and J. steps into the waiting room. She's wearing a black miniskirt and a cream-colored spaghetti-strap silk blouse, and she has a tan; she looks like her voice. "You must be James?" For the first time in my married life, an illicit sexual fantasy has come true.

A few moments later, I'm telling J. the highlights of my situation: married; monogamous—or, more precisely, celibate;

therefore feeling a constant desire to fool around, and hoping to decode this desire in a clinical setting so it won't threaten my marriage. Then I fall silent, try (unsuccessfully) not to look up J.'s skirt, and consider how to propose my preferred therapeutic option, which ideally will take place momentarily right *there* on the Freudian couch.

"What are you thinking?" she asks after a few weird, furtive minutes.

"This is a little awkward," I say. "I'd like to sleep with you." Everyone should have their own psychotherapist, it seems to me at this transcendent moment; universal mental health care; just to be able to say what's on your mind, *especially* if your mind is addled. It's so relaxing, if only for a reimbursable minute, to think that your thoughts, whatever they are, are *okay;* the *hot* talking cure!

"I see," says J. One can never be sure of anything in this world, least of all what a sexually attractive woman wearing a miniskirt thinks upon meeting an emotionally disturbed man who, a few moments after meeting her and closing the door on the two of them, has just proposed having sex, ideally then and there on her Freudian couch. But I'm pretty sure J. is freaking out. She seems to be recoiling in her chair, tugging down at her miniskirt in a hopeless attempt to cover more of her tanned thighs. I guess she's used to treating heterosexual women or gay men. It's almost poignant, really—to see J. grab for fabric that simply isn't there. Finally, she realizes her tanned knees aren't going undercover, and, like a true professional with a sexually deranged patient, she draws on page 1 of the clinical psychologist's playbook. "How does that make you feel?" she asks.

This is talk therapy! I read somewhere that a doctor's best friend is the placebo effect: If you *think* you're going to get better, you often do. Your mind controls your body. Well, I feel better already, thank you. Now if I can line things up so my mind controls *her* body and not just mine, I will walk out of here a new man. "It makes me feel good," I say, since she's asking, "the thought of having sex with you." Right there, on that couch, next to your bare, tanned legs. I keep this observation to myself, the underlying principle being that a hot psychologist likes crazy men—that's why she got into this business in the first place—but not *dangerous* men. I state the obvious, trying to soften the threat of an unwanted advance. "It feels weird to want to sleep with your shrink," I say, "but it's the truth." I look J. straight in the eye, under those lovely plucked eyebrows. They seem to arch slightly in alarm. But, according to *The Group,* a little fear in the bedroom can be a turn-on.

"You know it's never going to happen," says J. *"Don't you?"* She's trying to close the curtain on my fantasy and confirm that I live in what is generally referred to as "reality."

"Part of me knows," I say, so as not to flip her out. "But another part of me . . . doesn't." In other words, I'm an optimist. "In my fantasy life, anything's possible. And I have a highly developed fantasy life." The idea being, I know you don't want me to think you're easy; so let's go slow, take this one step at a time; talk about my fantasy life until you're comfortable manifesting it in reality.

"Let's talk about reality," says J., evidently not interested in taking things one step at a time. "Do you think we can get past your fantasies and get some real work done?"

"I don't know," I say, neglecting to refer to what I think of as our real work. "But I'd like to try."

"Good," she says, continuing her line of sadly sexless reasoning. "I think can I help you."

"How?"

"By talking about why you feel the way you do."

I know why I feel the way I do: I'm not having sex with my wife *or* my hot new therapist. What more is there to talk about?

"Usually impulses like yours mask some other need," she says. "If we can find out what that need is, maybe you can satisfy it in a way that's less threatening to your marriage."

"Are you saying my therapy is medically necessary?"

"Yes," says J., "I am."

That's when it hits me: This is the beginning of a *relationship*. I've really moved on from my old psychologist—his dim view of me as a normal human being with ordinary problems, versus an abnormal human being with special problems, thus *sick*. Which makes me feel great! After fifteen years, finally someone agrees: Monogamy is a mental-health problem.

TWENTY-FOUR

The Shape of Things to Come

I get to look at you
You get to look at me
We get to look at each other
And the whole darned thing is free!
—song for Julian, year sixteen

Jane is lying in bed, talking to our seven-and-a-half-month-old *fetus.* In utero.

He's kicking and squirming back.

They have a *relationship.* They're in the *same body.* He's *hers.*

I want him to be mine, and I don't feel pride of ownership talking to her belly. So I tell Jane, "What do you say we give him my name?"

Jane says, "He should have his own name." I can choose it, but it can't be mine.

"I guess that's okay," I say. "Seeing as he has my last name."

"What? He should have both our names," says Jane.

"You want to *hyphenate* him?"

"He's half you and half me," says Jane. "Why not?"

"It's ugly."

"Then let's give him my name," says Jane.

"Fine," I say. "We'll hyphenate him. Besides, he could change his name when he grows up. But he's never getting his foreskin back."

"You mean . . . *circumcise* him?" says Jane, like lopping off his foreskin is not a forgone conclusion.

"Of course," I say. The shape of my penis is the only thing left to give the guy, although it is my most important attribute.

"That's barbaric," says Jane.

"So is an uncircumcised penis."

"Do you have any idea what they actually do?"

I don't, not until the last night at the First Time Parents Workshop at the midwife clinic. We're sitting on yoga mats with the other first-time parents, when the instructor rolls in the video trolley, presses PLAY, turns off the lights, and walks out, followed by the other couples—and, of course, Jane—two by two by one, like a row of organic apple polishers.

I'm left alone in a room full of yoga mats flickering with the opening video title: *The Cruelest Cut.*

The sound track begins: *Thump . . . Thump . . . Thump . . . Thump*—a slow baby heartbeat with a little reverb.

Then the title dissolves to a baby on his back on a stainless-steel operating table, screaming and jerking in that palsied, newborn way.

Cut to the eyes of the surgeon, who's peering through the slot in his mask like an executioner.

Then to one of his hands, holding a scalpel, like a little guillotine.

Then to the other hand, holding the head of . . . a tiny penis. *THUMP-thump-thump-thump. THUMP-thump-thump-thump.*

Scalpel . . . penis . . . scalpel . . . penis . . .

THUMP-thump-THUMP-thump-THUMP-thump-THUMP-thump.

Scalpel . . . penis . . .

Aaaahhhhhaaaahhhhaaahhhhh! (The baby is) *Howling.*

It's like an animal rights video—with foreskin instead of veal.

After I stop dry-heaving, and then crying, I can see that I don't have the stomach to pass on the shape of my penis. In addition to not getting to pass on my first name or my last name. I want to be *reproduced.* To look in that crib and see a mini me. But it's not going to happen, and before my son is even born, it feels like something has died.

The door opens and everyone walks back to their yoga mats for the closing meditation.

The midwife lowers the room lights to create a womblike atmosphere. Then she asks us, in the darkness, to visualize the light each of us is soon to experience: It won't be long, she says, till our little ones are here! In the meantime, if we want to get to know him or her a little better—to experience firsthand what he or she is feeling *right now*—we can squeeze our earlobes. "That's the texture of a ripened womb," she says, having felt many such wombs over the years. "That's what a baby feels! The fruit is almost ready!"

Personally, I never wondered about the texture of a ripened womb—or even suspected that such a food/anatomy metaphor existed—until I signed up for the First Time Parents Workshop. Now, not only do I know what a ripened womb feels like; I know what a birthing mother looks like (having watched the *Pregnant Partners* video, which, were it sold at the sex shop on the corner, would qualify as graphic fetish pornography), in addition to knowing what a newborn boy sounds like when the head of his penis is lopped off (having just watched *The Cruelest Cut,* which would qualify as both pornography *and* pederasty, and perhaps vivisection).

But looking at videos of a bloody womb or its bloody infant fruit is one thing; actually feeling a uterus ripening on the side of my head, between my thumb and my forefinger, is something else altogether—something, in a word, nauseating. Or perhaps it's just the slice of Ray's Famous Original pizza I ate before the workshop. Whatever the reason, at the midwife's likening of my earlobe to a womb, I start dry-heaving on my yoga mat.

Jane whispers, "I think my water broke." The videos and/or meditation have had a physical effect on her, too!

"That can't be," I tell Jane, assuming Julian is on the same schedule we are. "The baby is due in six weeks."

"Something's wrong," says Jane, and she stands up on her yoga mat and walks out to find another midwife to examine her.

A few minutes later, that midwife walks in and leads me to the examination room, where Jane is sitting on a chair, crying.

"Jane was right," says the midwife. "Her water broke."

Jane looks up, red-eyed and stricken, and asks the midwife, "What do I do?"

The midwife says, "Can you walk?"

Jane says, "Yes."

The midwife says, "Turn right out the door on Fourteenth Street. Then right again on Seventh Avenue. Then left on Twelfth until you see a sign for Saint Vincent's. I'll fax over your paperwork." She says this in all seriousness, as though Jane is asking for directions, instead of help.

"I don't understand," says Jane.

I do, and I feel sick again. Not only do I now know what a ripened womb looks and feels like; I know what it means to actually *be* a womb: We are totally screwed.

"You have to go to the hospital," says the midwife. "Your baby's too early to be born here." The midwives handle only *ripe* fruit, in other words; green fruit is a case for the backup doctor— whom the midwives don't much like, and who told us he doesn't much like midwives when we met him in the "just in case the midwives flake and we need you to deliver our baby, let's get to know each other" session. Because, he said, like babies, midwives call only when they need you. But, unlike babies, they pay you, so he answers the call. Right now, I can see his point. I can't believe they're cutting us loose.

A few minutes later, we're walking down Fourteenth Street, both of us saying, "It's going to be fine," me to Jane, Jane to her belly—neither of us sounding very convincing.

Then I'm flashing insurance cards to the night clerk in the lobby of St. Vincent's.

We sit in a hospital room with a fluorescent ceiling, where a nurse straps a beeping fetal-heart monitor around Jane, and a weary-looking resident who's been up two days says, "Unless active labor begins in the next few hours, we're looking at a cesarean."

We're as far from a drug- and doctor-free candlelit water birth in a peach-colored birthing suite at a midwife clinic as you can get, thirty minutes after the closing meditation. It's worse than my worst worst-case scenario.

After examining Jane, the resident, says, "There may be meconium staining in the amniotic fluid. Fetal feces." In other words, *everyone's* scared shitless. "If this is meconium, the risk of infection goes up, and the doctor may want to get the baby out right away. If not, he may prescribe bed rest to give the baby more time to grow."

Jane starts talking to her belly again, looking on the bright side: "Stay in there, little guy. The doctor is going to give us bed rest."

We both nod off in the middle of the night to the sound of beeping monitors.

The next morning, the backup doctor, who hates the midwives who hired him to cover their emergencies, walks in. He reads Jane's chart, and then he examines her.

"I don't see meconium," he says. "But it could have been there last night. That baby has to come out."

Jane starts talking to her belly again, now trying to shift herself into labor. "I was wrong, little guy. It's okay to be born!"

The doctor leads me out to the hall.

"This is what happens when water breaks," he says. "Picture a graph." He points a forefinger and thumb at me, like he's holding a revolver. "The horizontal axis" (the barrel of the gun) "is the rate of infection. The vertical axis" (the hammer) "is elapsed time. For the first sixteen hours," he says, "the curve stays flat." He draws his other index finger toward his thumb, along the barrel of the gun in a friendly little line, meaning there is no infection. "At sixteen hours," he says, "it spikes," and he jerks his index finger straight up the hammer, meaning that at that point, my unborn son is going to die. "Jane's water broke eight hours ago," he says. "I'll see you at the end of the day." And he leaves.

No wonder the midwives don't like him. He could not be more unlike the leader of the First Time Parents Workshop. I've been told that to squish your earlobe during a discussion about ripened wombs is repulsive. But it's *way* more appealing than hearing about infant mortality rates. And Pitocin, a stimulant he tells me he's just injected into Jane to induce her labor, without having told either of us before, could potentially result in tremendous cramps and bleeding as the drug can act faster than her muscles can react.

It's times like these I understand Jane completely, why she chose midwives to begin with. I feel profoundly lucky she's in my life, connecting me to an entirely different way of seeing the world. Yes, the weight of our baby's life is on our doctor's shoulders. Yes, he's right to be cautious and to sometimes act without subjecting his medical thinking to a vote by amateurs. Every lifesaving drug has potentially life-ending side effects. But the moment we walked in here we were enveloped in institutional terror. Everyone seems to be acting not to embrace life, but to avoid death—and lawsuits. I can't even feel afraid anymore, much less excited. I'm numb.

I walk back into the hospital room, and for the first time in my life, I'm talking to Jane's belly like there's somebody on the other side. "Come on, little guy. You can do it."

Jane walks around the room, which, we learned in the workshop, stimulates the baby—and, we are learning right now, makes the fetal-heart monitor slip.

Making it appear that the baby is having a heart attack.

Which has a similar effect on the nurse at the nursing station who's monitoring the monitors. She runs in the room, screaming, "What are you *doing*? Get back into bed!"

So at the end of the day, when the doctor returns, the monitor's beeping, but Jane's not laboring.

Jane tells the doctor, "I can't labor in bed."

I say, "Maybe we should get a second opinion?"

The doctor says, "Who do you think will take you? Mother over forty. Baby premature. Probable meconium staining. You're untouchable."

I definitely hate you, I say to myself, looking at the doctor. I wish I didn't need you. *Why is so much of my life . . . like this?*

A few minutes later, a young Russian anesthesiologist drops by. "Something for you to sign," he says, "when you get a moment." Which, at that moment, as he walks out of the room, I can read is an "Accidental Death" waiver, indemnifying the young Russian anesthesiologist, who is now down the hall, and basically every employee of the hospital, wherever they are, against lawsuits from me should Jane die in a few minutes on the operating table—or later in the recovery room—"as a result of complications from . . ." It's easily the most terrifying document I have ever seen, far worse than a marriage license, or even a life insurance policy, which, like this waiver, is printed with both Jane's name and mine, unifying us in sickness and in health, and peppered with phrases like "sudden death" and "cardiac arrest" and "permanent brain damage" and "paralysis"—the same as the life insurance policy. Only I am being asked to sign this document a few feet (and a few minutes) away from a room in which all of these devastating consequences evidently occur, by a guy who conjures one of my father's scariest pieces of advice: "Someone always graduates at the bottom of his class. Make sure he's not your doctor."

The pre-op nurse appears with a razor, shaving cream, and iodine "to sterilize the operating theater," another anodyne turn of phrase that makes matters of actual life and death seem like hermetically sealed scenes in a daytime drama, denuded of all real consequence.

Finally, an orderly wheels Jane off on her stretcher.

I get to be with Jane once the surgery begins, I'm told. So I change into a surgical gown and mask and wait outside the operating room for the nurse. I can hear the instruments clanking and the monitors beeping and the doctors and the nurses murmuring and then, suddenly, Jane, screaming, "Where's James? Oh my God! You said he'd be here! James! James!"

I've lost control over everything now: my kid, my wife, my life. My job is to keep things stable, predictable. To perform under pressure. And I'm totally powerless.

So I sit on the floor and pray, out loud, which is when you really know you are not in control. "God," I say, "I don't ask you for much, except during turbulence in airplanes. But if you were going to give me anything else in life, please do it now. Please, God, let Jane live."

Then I say the same prayer for the baby. Which *really* scares me. Because I've just given away a second 911 to God to a complete stranger, which, if my calculations are right, I'll maybe get four or five of in my lifetime. It's the first time I really feel like a father.

Then a nurse appears and says, "Jane wants you." Like I can't hear Jane screaming my name.

The nurse presses a big steel button on the wall.

The operating room doors open, and I see the soles of Jane's bare feet twitching, and a team of doctors and nurses gathered around a hole in a sheet. It's hard to sort out where the iodine ends and the blood begins, but this is no theater; whatever it is I'm looking at dilates my skull. I look away and walk between Jane's gurney and the wall, my back to Jane, glancing at myself in the mirror of the scrub sink as I pass, at my eyes above my surgical mask. I look scared. Not the time, James, not the time, I tell myself. I move to the other side of the curtain that separates Jane's head from the doctors and the nurses, from the theater. I hold Jane's hand and tell her, "I'm here."

She's thrashing her head back and forth on the operating table like a wild animal in a trap, screaming, "They're cutting me open!" Evidently, epidural anesthesia is not all it's cracked up to be. Or maybe the young Russian anesthesiologist really is an idiot. Or maybe Jane is losing her mind.

As is the backup doctor. "You gotta get her under control, man!" he says, visible fear in his eyes. He's probably never seen anyone like Jane before and it's freaking him out. Just as Jane freaked out our marriage counselor Charles. She's an amazing, unique, discomfitting woman. Seriously, outside of Civil War docudramas, set back in the day where there was no anesthesia, who screams on an operating table?

"Jane," I say, "calming down will help the baby."

Jane says, "I can feel them inside me!"

I look back at the anesthesiologist. I really hope he didn't go to an offshore medical school.

Suddenly, the baby's wailing. Then he rises above the curtain, dangling from the doctor's hands, bloody and stunned.

Jane says, "Oh my God!"

We both start crying.

The neonatologists whisk him off, because he's six weeks premature.

"Stay with the baby!" says Jane.

"What about you?" A man's fundamental job is to protect his woman, who protects their child. How can I leave her?

"Stay with the baby!" Even paralyzed, drugged, and bleeding, Jane displays her protective instincts. The culmination of millions of years of biology, they are totally intact, and transferred, in a moment, to me.

I walk over to the incubator in the corner. The baby's on his back, surrounded by people listening to his heart and taking his footprints and squirting him with eyedrops. A nurse hands

me a pair of surgical scissors to cut off the last piece of his umbilical cord. This ceremonial ribbon cutting, an intiation into
fatherhood, feels as empty as cracking a bottle of champagne on
the side of a new ship, and also, strangely, as violent.

The baby's looking up as I carefully snip. We stare at each
other for the first time. And it's like looking . . . at somebody
else. I can see in his eyes, very clearly, that on the most fundamental level, he is who he is, already. And he is not me. I could
name him and maim him in my image, but I could never *junior*
him. Whoever he *really* is lies beyond my control. My only real
choice is to try to get to know him.

And right now, he looks angry, and scared. He's got doctors
and nurses poking pins into his fingers, shining lights in his
eyes, wiping off the coating he's lived in for months.

Then they're rolling him down to the neonatal intensive-care
unit and putting him under a heat lamp and weighing him and
turning him on his stomach like a five-pound, fourteen-ounce
rotisserie chicken. Meanwhile little two-pound crack babies are
undergoing withdrawal in neighboring incubators, screaming in
a frequency I've never heard, not even in horror movies; and
a nurse who's seen it all too many times is saying, "Some babies
weren't born to live."

I sit down in a chair next to the incubator and look at our
little guy through a porthole in the side. Then I reach in and slip
my little finger in his hand and he squeezes it and I sing him his
first song, "Silent Night"; then his second song, "Lucy in the
Sky with Diamonds." Then "Silent Night" again, because he
looks more holy than psychedelic. And when he falls asleep,
I slip my finger back out again.

I run up the stairs to Jane. When you're filled with this much joy, there's no time to wait for an elevator.

"Tell me about the baby," she says.

"He's very cute," I say. "He looks a lot like me. But he cries like you."

Jane says, "What should we call him?"

We still haven't agreed on a name, other than "not me." We figured we had six more weeks.

Many of the nurses here are Puerto Rican. I say, "How about Hunior?"

"Hunior?" says Jane.

"Junior, with a Spanish *J*."

Jane laughs for the first time since her water broke.

So Hunior it is. For a few days at least, until we get him home and I find out exactly who it is I've just fallen in love with.

TWENTY-FIVE

Stand-Up Husband

I want to go away, far from her
Make her feel like me
I'm in the place between to hurt her or to leave her
Let her be
—song for Jane, year sixteen

I'm sitting next to Jane on a little black couch in the office of Veronica, marital/sex counselor number twelve—the first eleven having terminated us for being hopeless, or having been terminated by us for telling us we were hopeless. Which has led us here, to the office of a woman who is still hopeful enough—or maybe just plain cruel enough—to begin the session by asking, in all seriousness, "How did your week go?"

I say, "Same as last week." Same as I said last week.

Jane says, "Don't blame me." Like she said last week.

I say, "It's your fault. You don't *do* anything."

Jane says, "I do *everything*. What little sex we have is *because* of me."

Which is true. *But* . . . "Why do you think we have so little sex to begin with?" I say, *"Because* of you."

Which leads Jane to scream, *"What*?" as enraged as she is genuinely confused, still not grasping the consequences of having met me when I was twenty-two years old, when fidelity was important in a stereo, not a relationship. I was too young to move in with her, even though I moved in with her.

Because Jane was—and is—lovely. Dirty-blond Ingrid Bergman hair, and innocent, wide-set, delft blue eyes, above a sharp nose and vaguely cruel Teutonic mouth, all sitting atop a regal neck leading to a fine body that looks great in and out of clothes. Which is especially impressive, given that she's had a kid. But we've been together over fifteen years, and done everything to each other so many times that we don't do anything anymore, unless Jane does something. And I want to do something about it, with someone else.

Veronica the marriage counselor, however, thinks lack of sex is a sign of deeper issues, as if there were something deeper than sex. "I think you two should separate for the summer," she says. "Take the narcotic, numbing effects of constant conflict out of your lives and see how you feel underneath. Have intimate relationships with yourselves."

In my case, this means spending the summer alone with me: a miserable human being. Which may be why I've resisted the idea of separating. But Jane and I agree—in itself a cause for hope—that twelve couples counselors over fifteen-plus contentious years represents the old college sweetheart try to keep things together, and that maybe it's time we take things apart.

So when we get home, I pack my clothes in a suitcase, take it out to the hallway, and move next door, to the studio that shares a wall with our apartment. We haven't broken through and combined the spaces yet, because renovating takes money. Which means making money. Which, in my case, means writing more marketing speeches for pharmaceutical executives, inventing lines like "This formula stops coughs cold." That was back when I worked on antihistamines. Now, having moved up the pharmaceutical food chain to erectile-dysfunction drugs, I come up with lines like "Every man deserves a quality erection." A noble sentiment I happen to agree with, now more than ever, but would rather leave unsaid. So as long as I'm separating from things that make me miserable, I call up my clients to say I'm booked for the summer. And I settle in to the unrenovated would-be master bedroom-cum-bachelor pad of an unemployed, undersexed, erectile-dysfunction expert.

The next morning, I wake up late and alone to the sound of Julian on the other side of my new front door. The marriage counselor's separation-with-a-baby formula is: *Contact = Conflict*. So the plan is for Jane to wheel Julian over every morning and knock, then walk back silently to *her* place.

I get up, open my door, and see Jane poking her head out of hers, next door, then look down to see my little boy lying on his back in his pram, smiling up at me. I scoop him in my arms, carry him inside, throw him on my bed, and kiss him till he screams. I'm hopelessly in love with Julian, same as I was with Jane when *we* were eight months old.

Later that morning, the two of us are sitting at the café on the corner, when two attractive women in clingy tops and spring skirts walk over to our table. One says, "Can I kiss you?" The other says, "I could eat you for breakfast." To Julian. They're talking to a baby who's getting more attention over breakfast than I've gotten my whole life, the little usurping bastard.

And here I've gone and separated from the only two things I'm good at: complaining about my marriage and my job. Complaining about my life. And with my life out of the way, what am I actually going to do?

Myself.

Then after a few days (there is such a thing as too much self-love), I sign up for a stand-up comedy class. I don't want to be a stand-up comedian. But I don't want to be a miserable husband and jealous father and an erectile-dysfunction expert. Doing what I don't want to do is how I get things done.

The class is held in a derelict commercial loft building in the west Fifties, one of those rent-by-the-hour places with a black metal sign in the lobby holding jumbled rows of white punch-in letters for each tenant, including "New York Comics Academy, 4th floor."

Upstairs, Professor Zach is standing by the door, greeting students as we walk in. Once we've all settled in at our desks, Zach starts the class. "Performers communicate on two levels," he says, "with their words and with their bodies. Let's begin by finding out what's your body language."

To demonstrate, Zach just stands there with his hands in his pockets, his eyes bugging out of his head, his body seeming to say, I need a thyroid doctor. He looks funny.

Then having demonstrated, he asks each of us to stand up in front of the class, one at a time, without saying anything—never having said anything to one another or ever seen one another until this evening—while the rest of us jot down our first impressions. There's a "Nordic home wrecker" with pert little breasts floating under an orange spaghetti-strap tank-top— "hot"; a blond "aerobics instructor" in black spandex and a jog bra—"hot"; a few young "dishwasher" guys or maybe "runaways" in soiled black jeans and heavy-metal T-shirts—"scary"; and me, looking—were Zach to ask me my impressions of myself— "understated yet distinguished" in khakis and a blue button-down oxford-cloth shirt.

The next week, Zach shares the findings in private student-teacher meetings in the corner of the classroom. When it's my turn, he calls me over and says, "Here are people's first impressions of you." And he hands me a list.

My name is printed across the top.

Underneath are five bullet points:

- Married
- Corporate
- Upper West Side
- Large Penis
- Gay

"There must be some mistake."

"No mistake," says Zach.

"Someone thinks I'm gay?"

"Actually," says Zach, fixing me with his bug eyes, "two people."

"That's half the class! Men or women? Maybe it's wishful thinking."

"I can't tell you," says Zach. "I'm just sharing information."

"What about 'Large Penis?'" I say. "Who said that? Please say Amber." The Nordic home-wrecker. "Or was it . . . a *guy*??"

"Whoever it was," says Zach, "you're coming across hung. Be happy for that."

Well, I'm not happy. I'm a miserable human being. Being told I'm a miserable *gay* human being, with no hetero appeal, to go with no wife, no job, and no sex.

Is that why they think I'm gay? Because I've only been touched by a man for a month? This is nothing new; this is *why* I separated.

I'll write them off!

I can't write them off—their other first impressions are right-on: I am married! I write for corporations! I live on West Eighty-third! My shoes are size twelve! And I never saw them looking at my feet and I never said a word! They know everything about me, like some circle of stand-up seers! I'm GAY!

That night, I walk home from the New York Comics Academy up Eighth Avenue, haunted, scared straight, trying to make eye contact with any woman who will look at me—frazzled executives leaving in black Town Cars, little cleaning ladies in pale blue uniforms arriving for the night shift—making my own list of impressions. While I was busy mastering the fine points of wife fighting and erectile dysfunction, my body was decomposing. Now instead of radiating sexual desire, the main thing it communicates is, You need a man.

The next morning, I call one up: Jacques, the personal trainer at the Pilates studio on West Fifty-seventh Street. I'd heard Pilates isn't real exercise (which I hate) yet somehow delivers real results (which I want), and therefore amounts to a fantasy workout.

It's true! When I walk into the Pilates studio, every mat is filled with a professional dancer wearing the cast T-shirt from her hit musical over a skintight leotard, looking at herself in the mirror, ankles hooked behind her neck, rocking, stretching, and, periodically, moaning. It's like the *Kama Sutra* on Broadway.

I tell Jacques, "I'll take the thirty-pack lesson book."

And I go back and forth to the studio, thirty times, religiously, like a man who worships the human body—oh, how I worship it.

By late August, when I look in the mirror at the studio, *The Beauty and the Beast, Chicago,* and *Mamma Mia* are looking back at me.

One day in the playground, a mother says, "You look different," before she kisses Julian. Because I do look different, and I feel different. I'm starting to like my real body, to want to share it with a real woman.

I'm starting to miss my wife.

I'm still struggling, however, with my stand-up routine as the final class approaches—a public performance at Caroline's Comedy Club on Broadway. I've never written stand-up before, and I don't know where to start.

"Write what you know," says Zach, like a bug-eyed comedy Yoda.

I know what it takes to stay married: twelve couples counselors, two apartments, and a separation agreement. And I know that if you somehow manage to have sex with your wife, and she gets pregnant and has a boy, you will experience penis envy: You will envy his, because of what he'll get to do with it when he grows up. Which makes you hope he turns out gay. (But I'll still love him even if he's straight.)

And that's what I tell the audience at Caroline's.

They understand.

I'm mystically hopeful and magically buff by the time the summer ends, and I meet Jane at marriage counselor number twelve one last time. We've been meeting Veronica once a week all summer long, and even making some progress; Jane's got me believing my problems are not all her fault.

Veronica asks us, "What have you decided?"

It's like being on a dating show for troubled couples, each of whom goes out with someone new and then compares that person to his or her partner. Only we've been dating ourselves for three months, there's a fifteen-year relationship with a kid on the line, and the host is a mental-health professional.

The counselor looks back and forth at the two of us, and says, "Are you going to end the separation? Or end the marriage?"

Jane and I turn to each other and smile, holding hands across the couch.

Partly it's pride, but the main reason I don't tell her that she's been right all along—that whoever Jane is, or we are, I was miserable long before I met her—is because at this moment I'm happy she is my wife.

TWENTY-SIX

Renaissance Man

Tadpole, glad pole
Sometimes you're a sad pole
Sometimes you're a mad pole
But always you're my tadpole
—song for Austin, year seventeen

Jane is half German, so her jokes are sometimes half funny—that is, not funny enough to be perceived as funny in the narrow, conventional, *American* sense of the word—and half deadly—that is, not deadly enough to be considered deadly serious. So I sometimes find myself wondering, Am I *not* getting the other half of the joke? Or did Jane just propose a seriously insane idea?

For example, Jane came home from the Buddhist grief counselor one day, announcing she'd made a major breakthrough in her post-traumatic hospital-birth therapy: To right the wrongs of Julian's birth in a hospital, she wanted to have our second child, Ben, in our living room. Was she joking? Or was she nuts?

Who would seriously propose having a baby in our living room? Which is also our bedroom, our dining room, and *every* room, as the three (and soon-to-be four) of us currently live in one room, because the other rooms, on the other side of the wall from the bedroom/dining room/every room, are being renovated. They are under construction, which starts with demolition. The sound track for Jane's (is she joking or is she nuts?) home birth—should it occur on a workday—would include jackhammers, regular hammers, and, depending on the intensity of her labor pains and the ethnicity of our laborers, Spanish- , Polish- and/or Israeli-accented murmurs from the other side of the bedroom/dining room/every room wall, or (if Jane really started screaming) total silence, which would be eerie (and an expensive waste of hourly rate labor) on a construction/demolition site. Not to mention that our part of the site—the part we live in—is about four hundred square feet. Divided by the soon-to-be four of us, that results in each of us having a little less space and far less privacy than your average federal prisoner in a supermax; the Unabomber has more room to stretch his shackled legs than we do.

Who would seriously suggest giving birth in *that*?

Jane would. She's looking at me plaintively, tears welling at the memory of Julian's difficult birth, fearless (or heedless) that she has just proposed an idea that—I'm no statistician, but narrow, conventional, American common sense would seem to dictate the outcome—has a statistically significant chance of failure, which in this realm of human behavior means *death* (hers and/or that of *our* baby). This would make Julian a motherless only child and me a widower at precisely the same moment, watching in stunned disbelief as the paramedic wheels away two body bags (one long, one short), then crying ourselves to sleep on the only bed in the bedroom/dining room/every room, a few feet away from the inflatable birth pool that has just killed half our family.

Immediately grasping this potential scenario, I say, "No!" Which is what I always say when Jane proposes an insane idea I later adopt. Following the birth of Julian, I've already learned how to deal with no crib—one bed for all of us; no weaning—two breasts for all of us; no vaccinations or medicine—homeopathic for all of us; no white bread; no sugar. But no doctor? No hospital? No way!

Jane pleads with me to support her. She's learned from painful experience that there are at least two ways to bring a baby into the world, and that the way of the hospital does not include peach-colored birthing rooms, bubbling hot tubs, Celtic harp music, and midwives who encourage you to walk around the clinic, then get on all fours and moan like a wild animal. In the hospital, you are not encouraged to be a wild animal—you are a patient. And you may not get on all fours, much less walk around on them. Instead, you must lie on your back in your bed, strapped to heart monitors—one for you, one for your baby, who, the moment you get out of bed and the fetal-heart monitor slips, appears to be in cardiac arrest, sounding the alarm at the nursing station, sending in the crazed, cardiac-accelerated nurse who screams, "Why are you *moving*!" This, in turn, immobilizes you *and* the baby, stalling your labor and forcing the backup doctor, who hates midwives (and the patients who love them), to wake up early the next morning and remove the baby from your body surgically, instead of waiting for the little guy to struggle on his own into the light. Which can leave fluid trapped in the baby's lungs, resulting in a breathing problem that can send that baby to the neonatal intensive-care unit, where he'll be put on a respirator and placed in an incubator, nestled amid rows of other screamy preemies, including the little crack addicts going through withdrawal (who *do* sound like wild animals; they are noisy even by newborn standards), each in a little plastic box under a heat lamp, like screaming squabs roasting during the dinner rush. This is what happened to Julian and Jane, sending her to a Buddhist grief counselor—for two *years*—for not being with her baby in his hour of need. She can't go through that again.

And when I think back on it, frankly I can't, either.

After we brought Julian home from the neonatal intensive-care unit, Jane would lie in bed at night, staring out the window in despair, repeating, "He was in an incubator, James"—which is where they put premature babies, so you can take them home alive—"*alone.*" As though Jane and Julian should have been incubated together in an adult-size box.

"But he's healthy, Jane!" I'd say, pointing out the obvious, trying to make her happy—without any success.

I can't take two more years of being the happy husband: nurturing the illusion that joy triumphs over adversity, carrying the weight of optimism. *She's* supposed to be the happy one in the relationship. I'm the one who gets to be filled with bottomless despair. And I *will* be filled with bottomless despair *if* I to agree to a home birth, since that will leave me a widower with a motherless child. *But* being filled with bottomless despair without the happy wife to take the edge off the pain is too much pain even for me.

So I split the difference. I tell Jane if I can be sure that the baby won't die and that she won't die (in that order—genetic love trumps romantic love), I'll make her happy by paying for a home birth. (Our health insurance company has a policy against paying for a home birth. Evidently the odds of a mother and/or child surviving it are so small, and the risk of liability lawsuits so great, the company would rather spend $30,000 for hospital care, than $5,000 at home.)

To be sure that *nobody* dies, I turn to the pages of *The Baby Book* by Dr. William Sears: Dr. Bill to his patients, America's pediatrician to his publisher, and, to his readers, the doctor with the ability to persuade mothers and fathers to share their beds with their newborns . . . and their toddlers . . . and their grade-schoolers. If anyone can convince me that a home birth is a good idea, it's the guy who convinced me I should sleep with a creature who wakes up every three hours, vomits and/or poops on me, and neutralizes what little chance remains of ever having sex again.

Sure enough, Dr. Bill writes that his own wife proposed having a home birth, which likewise caused him grave concerns. But he allayed them by setting up a temporary hospital in his house—essentially a homebirth MASH unit. It had a live-in obstetrician hired from the hospital down the street, in addition to Dr. Bill, a world-famous pediatrician who ran the hospital's pediatrics unit, because two doctors are better than one (and *much* better than none), it had a registered nurse, because one registered nurse managing the delivery is better than none; and it had two paramedics sitting in an ambulance in the driveway, just to be on the safe side. In all, Dr. Bill's home birth MASH

unit featured *five* conventional medical professionals, represent-
ing about one hundred years of collective experience dealing
with medical emergencies, plus an ambulance, not to mention
that Dr. Bill's wife was herself a registered nurse, capable of giving deeply informed medical feedback to her caregivers. Jane's
plan involved zero conventional medical professionals, no ambulance or transportation of any kind (unless you consider a
New York City taxi an emergency medical vehicle), and a patient
whose distrust of conventional medicine is so profound that she
refuses to use a thermometer on our son because she believes a
mother's intuition is better than a scientific instrument, *and*
that scientific instruments undermine a mother's intuition. After reading Dr. Bill, I can see no reason why any thinking
person should consider a home birth anything but dangerous
folly—conclusions sharply at odds with my desire to support
Jane's feelings. Thankfully, my fears vaporize amid the greater,
objective-fact-based terror instilled by Dr. Bill's sidebar on VBAC:
vaginal birth after cesarean. Given that Julian was delivered by
cesarean section, Ben would have to be a VBAC, which, according to Dr. Bill, is *the* most high-risk form of birth you can attempt; a woman who's been cut once can tear more easily the
second time around, "tear" being a euphemism for "bleed to
death," an anodizing phrase cut from the same medical cloth as
"operating theater." This perspective, I learn in some follow-up
research, is shared by the state of New York, which as far as I can
tell considers the VBAC procedure so dangerous, it's *against the
law* for a medical *doctor* to perform one *in a hospital*.

Jane is unmoved both by Dr. Bill's preparations and New
York State's prohibitions. Both are examples, she says, of the

patriarchy instilling in women fear of their own bodies, to make women (and their literally emasculated men, documented in *The Cruelest Cut* anticircumcision video) hostage to the fear-mongering, overcharging medical-industrial complex, which includes the people who invented thermometers to make you think you need mercury to know you have a fever! "Women have been having babies at home forever!" says Jane. "How do you think *we* got here?"

"By cesarean," I say, which is true in my case and also in the case of Julian. My son and I both owe our lives to the medical-industrial complex, without which not only *we* might have died during childbirth but also our mothers, which, of course, includes Jane.

Sometimes my facts are no substitute for Jane's feelings. And Jane says she has a good feeling about having Ben at home.

I walk to the hardware store and buy a hose, a faucet adapter, a sump pump, and an inflatable kiddie pool, which I inflate by mouth instead of with the foot pump. Yes, I hyperventilate to the point of passing out. But if my words and fears are going to be ignored, at least Jane and Ben will be surrounded by my protective breath. And (bonus!) the dulling effects of oxygen deprivation help numb the gurgling terror that I am making preparations for one and possibly two members of my family to die in my living room.

I'm in my underwear, sitting on the edge of the inflatable kiddie pool in my living room on Central Park West, suspending Jane by her armpits, doing a VBAC.

Jane is naked, and she is screaming "OH MY GOD!" at little baby Ben, who's naked and screaming back at her, suspended by his armpits by the home-birth midwife, while the doula circles around the four of us, taking pictures.

So far so good. One quick glance at Ben's shar-pei face and I can see through the wrinkles that the kid isn't mongoloid. Hideous, perhaps, but no uglier than any normal baby. It's a tremendous relief.

I'd had premonitions of Ben having Down syndrome ever since I looked at the risk tables for women Jane's age and saw that the odds of her having a baby with birth defects were one in twenty. It was statistically far more likely that I could join the army, invade a sovereign nation and not get killed; rob a bank and not get caught; or have sex with my old high school girlfriend and not get divorced—all things I'd scratched off my bucket list long ago as borderline crazy and in any case far too dangerous—versus Jane having a baby and us not getting devastated by birth defects. The more I thought about it, the riskier it seemed, until I became certain it was going to happen. We were in a little town in France, sitting at an outdoor café in the town square, when a British woman, who saw that Jane was a pregnant "older mother," told me how she had five sons and should have stopped at four; she knew she was too old and that asking for a daughter was asking too much of God. Sure enough, her last son had Down syndrome and it ruined her life, she said, and I should "prepare for the worst." It seemed clear that when we got back to the States, Jane should have a third-trimester abortion and donate the unborn kid's college fund to the reelection campaign of an extreme pro-choice congressman.

But when we got back home, she didn't have a third-trimester abortion; she didn't even have amniocentesis. I'd learned from Julian's trip to the neonatal intensive-care unit that a six-month-old, two-pound fetus—roughly Ben's current age and weight—could survive ex utero, even while undergoing withdrawal from crack, as many of the screaming preemies were. In other words, I'd seen for myself that Ben was viable. As for amniocentesis, which tells you whether or not the kid has birth defects, I figured if you're not willing to kill the kid, why find out he's going to ruin your life any sooner than you have to? Besides, I'd heard about some extreme pro-life parent group whose members made a point of adopting *only* Down syndrome babies. Worst case, Jane was currently serving as an unwitting surrogate mother for adoptive parents with a taste for birth defects.

But that does not seem to be the case. Ben does have black hair, a striking and somewhat disturbing feature, as it most assuredly does not run in my family, or in Jane's. But being cuckolded is way less bad than having to wipe your developmentally disabled kid's butt for the rest of his life. So I'm feeling pretty good, standing in my underwear, sloshing in the kiddie pool, amid Jane's moans and screams, and the flashbulbs from the doula cam.

Then Julian rushes in from the baby-sitter in the hall and asks, "Does the baby have a wiener?" (No amniocentesis means no prior knowledge of gender.)

I start doing the new-dad math: one wiener. "You've got a little brother." With ten toes, ten fingers, two eyes, two ears—check, check, check, check—and a mouth that doesn't breathe right. Just like Julian's. Meaning, Ben needs to go to the hospital, just like Julian . . . which will send Jane back to the Buddhist grief counselor and—quite possibly—over the edge. Taking me with her. And I don't *want* to go with her!

So we all decide, for our own various reasons, that the prudent course with Ben is "wait and see."

"Many times," says the home-birth midwife—she's the authority figure in the room, standing there in combat boots and a peasant dress—"breathing problems like these naturally resolve themselves."

Three hours later, the problem is not resolved, even though the midwife has Ben on oxygen.

So I call Julian's pediatrician, the past president of the New York College of Pediatricians, just to make sure that what we're doing isn't crazy. When he calls back, I tell him what's happening: "I've got a newborn baby in my living room. He's got a breathing problem. And it's lasted for about three hours."

The pediatrician says, "Are you serious?" (Sounding like I did after Jane first proposed the home birth—clearly not sure whether this is a half-funny, half-deadly joke or a deadly serious statement of fact, with potentially deadly consequences.)

"Yes," I say, as ashamed as I am desperate.

"That's *crazy*," he says. Like I didn't know. "Get him to a hospital!"

"Just like a doctor," says the midwife, who's been listening in, after I hang up.

There's a pall in the room, or at least in my head, as it sinks in that my worst fears have been confirmed: What we're doing is nuts.

So like any responsible parent who has just been told by the past president of the New York College of Pediatricians that he is endangering the life of his newborn child, I seek a second opinion, from the 1-800 help line of my health insurance company. It's right on the back of the card. And unlike a home birth, it comes with my policy. (You can get free medical advice after the fact about the high-risk adventures the company wouldn't pay for to begin with.)

A registered nurse comes on the line. I tell her what's happening: "I've got a newborn baby in my living room. He's got a breathing problem. It's lasted for about three hours."

She says, "That is the craziest thing I've ever heard! And I've been a nurse for twenty years! Get him to a hospital!"

"Just like a nurse," says the midwife, almost on cue, discounting "Western medicine" the way Western medicine discounts midwifery; health-care providers, heel thyselves!

So I seek a third opinion—from someone more enlightened. Someone who can see beyond conventional medical practice, and the fear of medical malpractice. Someone, suggests the doula, like the half Lakota Sioux Indian. He graduated from Stanford Medical School at twenty-one, and let his son self-wean at seven . . . years. Just as Jane wants to do with Julian, and now Ben. He's a freak. Our kind of doctor.

So I get him on the line and tell him what's happening: newborn, living room, breathing problem, three hours.

He says, in this preternaturally calm half Lakota Sioux voice, "Put the phone up to the baby's mouth, please."

I do.

"His breathing sounds a little rapid," says the medicine man. "I'd be glad to see him."

It's Sunday night. Eleven o'clock. Well past office hours. And it's raining. Not a good time to be out on the town with a newborn baby whose lungs may be about to fail and a father whose sanity is even more fragile. "Where?" I say, hoping he'll say, *Your place! Of course!* The notion of an American *Indian* doctor giving rise to fantasies of house calls, like a medicine man on the prairie, oh, a century ago. I really do live much of my life in the amber of child-like expectation, assuming the world will meet my needs, which in moments like these makes it abundantly clear: Adapt or die.

"In the lobby of the Gershwin Hotel." He's giving a late dinner lecture to medical students.

I bundle Ben in a blanket, the doorman hails a cab, and Ben and I ride downtown in the backseat for the big night, Ben screaming and jerking in that palsied, newborn way, me kissing him on the forehead, trying to calm him, wishing someone would appear to kiss me.

When we get to the Gershwin, it turns out to be a hipster hotel; they play trip hop and emo on the sound system. Ben and I stand there grooving in the corner, me telling the occasional security guard, "We're fine, thanks."

Finally, a little guy with a ponytail taps me on the shoulder and says, "Follow me."

He leads us across the street, through the side door of an office building, up a flight of stairs, and into a medical examination room.

"Put the baby on the table, please," says the medicine man. Then he listens to Ben's heart and lungs, shines a light in each eye, and snaps a finger in each ear. "The sound you are hearing is whimpering. It should be gone by morning."

I've never seen this guy in my life. I don't even know his name. The only thing we have in common is a doula who takes photographs at home births. If he's wrong, that's the end of my family. But if he's right and I ignore him and take Ben to the hospital, quite possibly that's the end of the mother of my family, psychologically.

So I look in the medicine man's eyes a long time . . . and I trust him.

I bundle Ben back up in the blanket, walk downstairs, and try to catch a cab. Hard enough in the rain—everybody else wants a cab, too—but with a squirming newborn in your arms, it's impossible. When the driver pulls up and sees that I'm dripping wet and that one of Ben's premature little limbs is poking through a hole in the soaking blanket, his eyes visibly dilate in a "I've never seen this level of human depravity, and I am a war refugee!" way, and he locks the doors and speeds off, leaving me standing in the middle of the street, one arm holding Ben like a football and the other extended to where the car door used to be. Then a homeless guy crawls out of his cardboard box on the sidewalk and stumbles drunkenly through the rain, holds out his hand to me, and asks for money. Until he sees my blanket jerking and hears Ben mewing, and he says, "What kinda shit is that?" He's looking at me like I'm the devil, lurching away, visibly terrified, double-timing it across the street, having seen something so alarming, he'd rather go cold turkey than beg for Thunderbird. I stuff Ben in my jacket, turn my back to traffic, and finally catch a cab home.

In the apartment, I give Ben to Jane. And for the first time in his life, he nurses, and the two of them fall asleep, with me watching over them, praying the medicine man was right.

The next morning, Ben opens his eyes and gurgles. He's fine. Julian's back from the baby-sitter and on the bed, comparing wieners with the new guy. (It starts early.) Jane's in a nightgown, lying next to them, beatific.

"That was the most amazing experience of my life," she says. "Let's do it again!"

As though I'm not there, slumped in a chair in the corner, catatonic, staring out the window at a little family of pigeons gathered under the eaves of a neighboring building, hiding from the rain. Didn't I learn anything the first time around? That taking a kid to a hospital . . . is okay? That Jane's melancholy—and my fear of it—are less important than a child? I haven't slept in two days. I don't know that I'll sleep tonight. The only thing that seems clear to me is that I just risked Ben's life, and my own mental health, to save Jane.

TWENTY-SEVEN

Nuclear Meltdown

What do other people know that we don't?
—While driving with Jane in the only car along the
Grand Corniche, before seeing an enormous, asteroid-
sized boulder in the middle of the highway.

Sometimes I just get tired of protecting people's so-called mental health. Why is it *my* job to keep someone from realizing they're crazy? Because I hope they'll do the same for me? Well, you know what? I don't need it anymore. I'm fine being nuts. After my life, my marriage . . . I've earned the crazy merit badge.

So I get up from the visitor's stool in Kate's room and walk down to the end of the baronial hall, past the huge mahogany doors, their brass knobs occasionally hung with the handmade cards with colorful stickers of butterflies and flowers that poetically, innocently warn, Please don't come in; I'm dead.

I get to the family room: a formal, quiet space full of wing chairs and mahogany tables, throw rugs and pillows, porcelain decorative vases and brass andirons—furnishings and accoutrements befitting the oil baron who used to call this place home.

My mom, dad, brother, sister, and aunt look up at me from different corners of the room for news. Roger has Kate's medical power of attorney, and he has used his power to banish them all here, citing the reason that they are toxic to Kate's health—and though her life expectancy could be measured in hours, or certainly days, it's never too late to detox. I'm serving as the ambassador, just returned from a land they no longer are welcome to visit, except at the pleasure of the Power. I presume the Power will grant Kate her wedding wish: to invite whom she wants to invite to her wedding. Even though I am sure that every single one of her guests will mistake her wedding wish for a curse. I can't wait to tell them about it! Bad news is like good news that way, sometimes: Both hold the fascination of the rare and the extreme. Especially when you're the only one who knows the news!

"Go home," I say, spooling out the good bad news, nursing my dark little secret. "Get dressed." You can see the confusion on the faces that are open to at least the possibility that all people aren't screwing you all the time: We already *are* dressed. What does *that* mean? Versus my dad's, whose eyes always seem fixed on a target that only he can see. I don't think much of most people, son, he once told me, 99.9 percent of the time I'm right. "There's gonna be a wedding."

Poof. I don't know whether it's actually possible to see pupils dilating in real time, but that's how it looks to me. And I think I hear their hearts beating faster and the blood rushing to their temples, to their brains, to their voice boxes.

"You have *got* to be kidding?" says Corinne. Eyes ablaze at the prospect of Kate's wedding just like they looked as we strangled each other at Corinne's wedding. Weddings get her excited!

"How did Long Hair get a marriage license?" asks my dad, instantly grasping the primary obstacle to a deathbed union, like the problem-solving bomber pilot he once was (the solutions to most problems being to drop bombs), to his credit referring to Roger by the least offensive of his family monikers—Long Hair—the other two being the Moron and the Aborigine, a word that in my family—though Roger is Australian—does not connote native person. My dad's favorite book is the New Testament, so with dawning Christian rage, he answers his own question, "The preacher!" Who's been coming around to Kate's bedside each night, trying to get a deathbed conversion. "That son of a *bitch*!"

The appealing thing about unbridled fury is that it's like any passion—sex, drugs, rock and roll: Once you free yourself from the possible human consequences of overindulging in it and just surrender, it's fun! The social worker told me, in so many words, let water seek its level. That means I get to be part of the deluge! Why try to inject a sober note of sanity when it's so intoxicating to be insane!

I say, "Maybe Roger is trying to adopt a baby, Dad!" So that Roger can inherit Kate's share of the family trust, as then he would be the *surviving custodial parent* of their child. Kate's share cannot be bequeathed to a childless husband, much less to a mere boyfriend. If he really is marrying her for her money, *they have to have a kid together*!

My dad says, "I didn't think of that, son!"

"I didn't think of that, either!" my brother says, with a mixture of concern and envy that I've uncovered a conspiracy they overlooked.

Which I have!

Finally! As the baby of the family, I've spent my whole life being usurped by everyone else's superior capacity for the dark estimation of human nature. They're always the first to threaten one another, file lawsuits against one another, and divorce one another. Until now. This is how Amundsen must have felt when he got to the South Pole ahead of Scott!

Suddenly, my aunt Jenny, the practical one in the family, says, "What adoption agency would let a baby go to a moron and a drug addict dying of cancer? I think it's going to be hilarious when the creature finds out he's not inheriting a thing."

Pop goes the conspiracy theory.

Poof goes Amundsen.

I am Scott: wrong in my calculations; second place; dead in the water—or on the ice—again!

My mom, her twin, says, "He's too stupid to figure that out."

Corinne, deeply imprinted by my father on the one hand and on the other by years of watching Marilyn Monroe films, accesses her inner breathy bottle-blond bombshell and says, "I don't care if you are a hideous moron. You can't help it if you're born stupid and ugly. What matters is what's inside." This is the president of Facade speaking, sounding like Norma Jean Baker reading for the part of Mother Teresa. "And what's inside, I assure you, is pure . . . *evil!*"

Now *that's* my sister!

I've got a nice chaos buzz going. I've dropped the deathbed-wedding bomb. Poured on the incendiary adopt-a-kid-to-steal-the-family-money grab. And totally vaporized my life—my own concerns—replacing it with narcotic, deeply distracting toxic fury. Who cares that my sister is days or hours from death? Who cares that I have two boys back home with chores, teeth, home-work, and a taste for breast milk? Who cares that in my freezer right now, tucked under the organic raspberries, Jane keeps a frozen human organ awaiting burial?

My dad turns to me and says, "Now, how are you and Jane get-ting along, huh?"

TWENTY-EIGHT

Sex on Ice

I've got a purple telephone
And it rings when I'm alone
And it's ringing more and more these days
—song for Jane, year eighteen

I'm sitting at one end of a rustic table, at a little dinner party up in Copperfield, a progressive community in upstate New York where Jane and I have rented a house, having sold our apartment in New York City in the hopes of maybe raising Julian and Ben up here, in an even *more* progressive setting than the Upper West Side of Manhattan. Where, you may not know, it is *not* okay to breast-feed a three-year-old child in public, at least not during a battle scene in act 1 of *Henry V* at Shakespeare in the Park. The usher might tell you, "I'm sorry, but the director says the actors are freaking out and if you're going to keep doing *that,* you'll have to leave." In Copperfield, during the fall fair, I personally witnessed a fifty-something gray-haired woman sitting on a farm bench, flipping open the breast flap of her Mennonite canvas bib dress to nurse her four school-aged children, one after the other. On the other hand, our first rental house up here was haunted by the landlord's dead husband, who sat in the antique barber chair in the master bedroom, facing all of us on the first night—we were cowering together in the master bed (when a family co-sleeps, one ghost can cover a lot of ground)—so the morning after we moved in, we had to move out, because we couldn't find an exorcist. So it's not *that* progressive up here. (Yes, I know, to some a man who sees a specter can seem superstitious, therefore limning his perspective with suspicion. Not everyone has the sensitivity to see specters. We each have different gifts, and sometimes a man and a woman with similar gifts marry, producing children to whom those gifts pass, one of whom says, "Dad, this place gives me the creeps." Thus creating a situation where what some might think of as a subjective metaphysical experience is in fact as plain as the nose on a scary ghost's face. All to say, in many ways, Jane and I were made for each other.)

Anyway, we're at the local midwife's, or at one of the local midwives' (where there's progressive smoke, there's progressive fire): an uninsulated cottage, which I find, frankly, depressing. Who wants to wear a sweater at the dinner table? (Evidently, everyone in Copperfield.) On the other hand, the midwife does have a bottle of some kind of fermented beverage, *other* than kombucha—mushroom champagne, perhaps the most repulsive carbonated beverage I have ever tasted—suggesting we may have something in common. The problem being, it's in the other room, tucked away on the counter, behind the jars of spelt and quinoa, progressive versions of wheat and rice. Everything here seems so fraught with meaning. I wish I could just have a glass of wine without measuring its carbon footprint or political ramifications. But at least one *can* have a glass of wine here, eventually, maybe. And the cottage has a lovely view, overlooking a pristine meadow that the local farm uses to graze its local cows.

This is locavore country: People who eat local, buy local, *think* local. Recently, for the first time in my life, I ate a meal comprised of ingredients provided by people I had actually met: fabulous steak and potatoes from Pat at the Columbia Valley Farm, just down the road; excellent arugula grown by Monica, the Quaker, in Chatham; and for dessert, apple crumble, made with amazing apples grown by Jill and Jerry. Okay, so maybe it's insane to bury a bull's horn filled with fermented manure by the light of the full moon once a year, before planting season begins, to temper the earth—a biodynamic farming principle that Jerry (and most of the farmers around here) swear by. But whatever the reason, his apples are the best I have ever eaten. And the bottom line for me is, if I can satisfy (a) my gluttonous desires, (b) my competitive desire to be onto the next cool thing before others discover it, and (c) my vague yearnings to be enlightened, I can (a) eat well, (b) eat better than you, and (c) eat in a way that saves the world—which I could never do in Manhattan. I think I might find something here I can actually sink my teeth into.

From the far end of the dinner table I overhear Jane telling our new neighbor Everett about Ben's *placenta*. Not your normal dinner party topic, perhaps. But this is not your normal dinner party—no one seems in the least surprised, or to have suffered the least loss of appetite; they just go on eating, like we're talking about the Yankees.

"Originally," Jane tells Everett, "after the home birth . . ." She wanted to bury Austin's placenta in Central Park and plant a fertility tree on top of it. "Like they do in Africa," she explained when the two of us were first discussing this. Jane had learned about this practice in divinity school, in a course on fertility cults. Then *somebody* warned her that the burying of human remains in Central Park was probably illegal—that somebody was me—and that even if the park police didn't catch us digging a grave, they'd definitely notice the funeral Jane wanted to hold around Ben's placental grave site. "Not if we did it at night," Jane said to me at the time, before realizing her friends would not come to a funeral in the dark.

Which is how Ben's placenta ended up in a little clear plastic tub in our freezer, for *three* years, including the blackout, when it thawed and refroze, turning from red to maroon to brown behind multiple layers of ice crystals.

That's where it remained until the day we packed it on ice and drove it up here to Copperfield, where it's sitting tonight in our rental freezer. Until we can buy a house with a little plot of land and hopefully lay Ben's placenta to rest once and for all.

"James . . ." says Jane to Everett and now to the rest of the guests, all of whom are listening to her at this point, blithely munching away, "James is upset that Ben's placenta is still in our freezer. James . . ." says Jane, "James thinks I'm weird."

I'm familiar with the practice of women using public forums to air their private grievances with their men in order to gain allies in their spousal combats because they feel outnumbered at home. My mom, for example, went to the commanding officer at the air force base to complain about my father, General Eisenhower's personal pilot (because she could not persuade my father to agree with her).

Even though I wasn't there I can understand why a housewife would act this way: How are you going to win an argument against a guy that powerful without allies? Okay, so that means turning his bosses against him, and therefore, as he is the breadwinner, against your family. But such is the price of winning wars on the home front. Jane has used this technique countless times over the years in our marriage, enlisting family and friends and neighbors and marriage counselors and sometimes even complete strangers in a variety of domestic campaigns, often with great success. Like any vanquished competitor, I look back on her victories, which are therefore my losses, with a mixture of regret (coulda, woulda, shoulda), anger (the ref didn't see her stepping out of bounds) and, truth be told, grudging admiration (maybe she *was* right).

But this time, it seems to me, she's gone a bridge too far. Who would think *I'm* weird for not wanting a human organ in my freezer for three years? Apart from Starlight, that is, our former neighbor in the city, who is our new neighbor up here. She had *two* placentas in her New York City freezer, citing the same reason Jane froze one: "Where am I supposed to bury them?" When I asked Starlight why she felt she had to bury them to begin with, and, in any case, if she didn't think freezing her placentas for years was odd, she said, "Women have been doing it for centuries!" I said, "There haven't been freezers for centuries, Starlight." That, more or less, was the moment I knew Starlight would never invite me back to her nursing circle, where I was privileged to see the expressions on the nursing mothers' faces as she passed around her portfolio of black-and-white nude self-portraits.

Part of me recoils in shame when my emotional laundry is being washed in public, at a dinner table, in front of more or less complete strangers. But a bigger part of me sees the wisdom of publicly fighting private matters—all while seeming *not* to fight! I can have my organic quinoa salad *and* eat it, too: This is a whole dinner table of potential new allies! With any luck, by this time tomorrow, they'll persuade Jane to free up three quarts of space in my freezer and place the placenta-filled plastic tub in the landfill.

But when Jane says *I* think *she's* weird for freezing a human organ for three years, everyone at the table turns to me with a suddenness and force that, were their heads the size of palm fronds, would feel like someone just turned on a fan: three single moms who left their mates or were left by them before moving to Copperfield; Everett's wife, Sage; Jane; and Everett, the only other man in the house, whom I lock eyes with, man-to-man, to let him know we're in this together.

It's a lesson I learned while watching Mick Jagger at a Rolling Stones concert when I was a kid: Start with one person, focus all your energy, and build heat that radiates to others. Like frying ants with a magnifying glass, or starting a campfire. It's the kindling effect of audience development. Jagger was singing to me, and by the time he finished, I was so overheated, I passed out in the stands. Which could have been because there were eighty thousand people around me and it was one hundred degrees outside, but still.

So I'm looking at Everett, hard, hoping he feels the heat.

When Everett takes a bite of *quark*—a progressive cheese by-product he's contributed to the dinner party (he's an organic-cheese maker)—and he says, very matter-of-factly, "We ate our placenta."

What would Jagger do? I wonder, If he found himself at a dinner table with not just one, but two people who willingly consumed a human organ, chewing and swallowing a piece of meat that originated inside one of their bodies, seeing their viscera as most of us see a garden patch: a source of fresh food. I say the only thing I can think to say, fingertips slipping off the last ledge of reality in the room. *"Why?* Why would you do that?"

"It seemed like the right thing to do at the time," says Everett.

"Says who?"

"My friend on the mountain in Santa Fe. She actually recommended it," says Everett. "And I revere her in all things spiritual. She even gave me the recipe: pan-roasted, in cumin."

"Curry!" says Everett's wife, Sage. "Don't you remember? It was curry, Everett!" she insists, correcting him like he's forgotten her birthday, or what happened on their first date; as though the issue is the memory of the spice (when you are named after an herb, this is not splitting hairs), not the quasi-cannibalism. She's arguing with him like a nonprogressive spouse, which at this point is the only behavioral landmark at the table.

"Curry. Cumin. It was something with a *c,"* says Everett. "Whatever it was, it was delicious."

I ask him how it tasted. I really want to know. I've never met anyone who's eaten part of the human body. And with any luck, I'll never have this chance again.

He says he can't describe it.

"Try," I say. "You're in the food business."

"Well," says Everett, rising to the occupational challenge, "it was more tender than filet mignon, but not at all mushy like liver." And then, in a reverie, he adds, "It was the most delicious piece of meat I've ever eaten."

"You just fried it straight out of Sage?"

"The home-birth midwife doubled as our butcher," says Everett.

"She removed the umbilical cord and filleted the meat. I did the rest."

"Wow," says one of the single moms, Annie, Jane's franny (friend and nanny), who lives by the credo *What would a raccoon do?* It keeps her in sync with nature. "That is so beautiful." Everett is the incarnation of every Copperfield woman's dream. Not only does he not shy away from her most private part; he cooks it and eats it. Like a man. Or, apart from the cooking, a raccoon.

"See," says Jane, from the far end of the dinner table, "it's totally natural."

"In Copperfield," I say.

"Totally," says Sage. "It's the only meat you don't have to kill to eat."

I'm planning on raising my kids among these people. It takes a village. *They're it.* So I go around the table and ask the single moms one by one, "Did you eat your placenta?" I just want to get to know my new neighbors.

The first single mom, Annie, says she didn't have enough support. She was alone, in the hospital, having an emergency cesarean. "The nurses took my placenta away," she says, forlornly, like they'd kidnapped her baby. "But today," she says, "I think I'd be strong enough to eat it."

The second single mom says she adopted her baby, so there was no placenta to eat. "But I would have if I could have."

The third single mom says that eating human organs is not her style. She buried her placenta in her backyard, under a fertility tree. Sadly, the fertility tree died when she went away on vacation and the neighbor forgot to water it. But another neighbor did once borrow her food dryer to make placenta jerky. So she knows where Everett is coming from.

I've given up my life to be here tonight. Quit my job, sold my apartment, left it all behind to give me and Jane—and Julian and Ben—a fresh start. I need to make it work. So it occurs to me, Maybe Everett is right. Maybe I'm just being narrow-minded. Maybe a human placenta really is a delicious piece of meat. Notwithstanding that it's medical waste and it should be burned and there isn't enough curry in the world to cover the taste of that thing. *What am I thinking?*

So I make a joke—to get my bearings. "With Jane's permission," I say, "I'd like to invite you all to dinner at our house the next time. You bring the wine. We'll serve placenta. If Everett will do the honors of cooking."

No one makes a sound. Up in Copperfield, a placenta's no joke. It's food, and they think I've really invited them over to my house to eat one. And judging by their silence, they are actually considering it. Then Everett looks at the kids running around the living room and says, "How *old* is Ben?"

"Three . . . *years!*"

"James," says Jane, far from the far end of the dinner table, visibly embarrassed, stacking dirty dinner plates to calm herself, evidently believing, just as our new neighbors believe, that I have seriously suggested we all eat a three-year-old frozen piece of her body. "A placenta should be eaten fresh," she says. Like she's lived in Copperfield her whole life.

One of us is a long way from home.

TWENTY-NINE

One Last Family Photo

Death isn't black, it's gold
—song*

For all its eccentricities, a deathbed wedding is still a wedding. You need an officiant, vows, music (all of which are coming tonight, compliments of the fundamentalist preacher who's been seeking a deathbed conversion from Kate for the last few days), food, drink, flowers, and clothing.

Corinne and I drove to Mueller's, a pastry shop that, like many businesses in Houston, is housed in a strip mall. Since Easter is the next major holiday, Mueller's shop windows feature paper cutouts of bunnies and eggs and grass. Corinne, having given more than her share of parties and weddings, ordered a few boxes of their best petits fours.

Then we drove to Whole Foods to buy the flowers and the organic vanilla ice cream and frozen cherries, which I had been

---

*by Lawrence Fishberg

feeding to Kate all week, late at night, when she woke up. Whole Foods also sold wine, but when I put a bottle of fancy champagne in the basket—I knew Kate cared about the label—Corinne told me she had a cellar's worth of fancy champagne at home, gifts from suitors who didn't realize she doesn't drink and that as an independent girl without independent means, she either regifts or returns gifts for cash or store credit—unless it's jewelry.

Hence the visit to the watch shop next door to Whole Foods to confirm the value of the watch her recently dumped boyfriend gave her before the Big Fight. "He told me to back my 'fat ass' up to the three-way mirror and see what the rest of the world saw," said Corinne as we walked into the store. "So I told him, 'Listen, Tits!'" (Evidently he suffered from gynomastia, aka male breasts.) "'Your boobs are bigger than mine!'" And she took the watch, and the keys to his Jaguar.

That night, at ten o'clock, wearing the dark suit I had reluctantly packed in New York, thinking I might have to wear it once, I walk into room 202 at the hospice with the rest of my family:

Corinne is perfectly groomed in a sensible calf-length black summery dress, wearing more makeup than your average kabuki dancer—just as you'd expect the president of Facade to be wearing—yet looking entirely natural, like this is how she wakes up every morning.

My mom is equally well turned out and has a perfectly made-up face, which, with all due respect to the plastic surgeon, is a tribute both to my mom's natural beauty and Corinne's makeup lessons and Facade products. (Yes, my mom demands a discount on the products—wholesale plus 5 percent—but she does buy a lot of them, *and* she tells her friends.)

My dad is sitting in his wheelchair, looking like a natty charismatic cross between the country-and-western star Roger Miller—golden stretch trousers with a yellow golf shirt, wrapped in a beige-and-cream-checked houndstooth jacket with brown suede elbow patches, amber-hued aviator sunglasses and a scraggly beard—and, Orson Welles in his twilight-of-the-gods, "We will serve no wine before it's time" well-fed television spokesman phase.

My brother, Earl, is here, down from Austin for the night, in one of the bespoke suits he dressed to look the part of the baron's daughter's husband, twice.

My mom's twin sister walks in, looking pretty much like my mom but in a muumuu—or is that a caftan? Whatever the garment is that both Elizabeth Taylor and Zero Mostel (or Orson Welles) could wear interchangeably, that's what my aunt is wearing, only with more jewelry than La Liz. "I like your hair like that," says my aunt to Corinne. "I wouldn't say it if I didn't mean it. I'd just keep my mouth shut. I got into an argument today with this fat pig down at the bridge studio," she says, by way of nothing, proving that she is both sincere and brutal, as well as utterly oblivious to the underlying reason why she is wearing a muumuu.

Earl says to me, "How many ways can you call someone fat?" It's a legitimate question. *Fat* is to the women in my family as *snow* is to Eskimos: a phenomenon that requires dozens of different nuanced names to describe its particular variation.

Princess Grace, Kate's patron lover dealer, is here, dressed in lovely sublime navy-and-pearl understatement—dark shift, exquisite choker, patent leather pumps—having delayed her return to London. She lives next door to Claus Von Bulow, the socialite who was acquitted of injecting his wife into the coma from which she never awoke. "He's a lovely man," Grace had told me in her typically inscrutable way, betraying no hint either of irony or earnestness; just a statement of fact. This before promising that she would consult with me before euthanizing Kate. I love Grace. I really do. But as Claus von Bulow would be the first to admit, the rich are not like you and me.

Kate's asleep in her bed in the corner, as usual.

So we stand or sit around and wait for Roger to arrive.

My dad says, "Where is Long Hair?"

Corinne says, "The Moron probably forgot how to get here."

My mom says, "What do you expect from an Aborigine?"

Grace—whom my mom suspects of sleeping with him—says nothing.

I finally say, "Whatever we think of Roger—and I'm not crazy about the guy—I think he's marrying Kate because he loves her, and he wants control. Of her *body*. Her ashes mean more to him than they do to us."

My dad says, "Long Hair doesn't love her any more than my cat, son. It's all about the money. So put your antennas out just a little bit farther and see what you can pick up." And he points his meaty index fingers up on the top of his head, like antlers, before resting his huge farm boy hands back on his thighs.

"Where are Rhonda and her rodent?" says my mom, referring to Roger's mom and her lover. To be late is worse than being a lesbian.

"Maybe the black flapping vultures flew home, Mother dear," says Corinne.

"Let me tell you something about Long Hair," says my dad. "His mother's she . . . is a he . . . wearing a wig."

"I don't know, Dad. She *is* a little mannish, but . . ." I say, trying to empathize while changing the subject.

"She's not a woman, son! Maybe she's an . . . *armaferdite*," he says, his volume audibly lowering on the last word, sotto voce— not from discretion, I suspect, but from self-doubt. My dad is a brilliant man, perhaps even a genius. He was among the best pilots in the Air Force, distinguished enough to fly the man who managed World War II, at the point in history when it was clear Eisenhower would be the next president of the United States. But you can hear the poignant gaps in his education in his command of sexual slurs. "At the least," he says, confidence (and volume) returning, "she's a major oddball!"

I walk across the room to get away from my dad, and sit down in a window seat next to Kate.

My dad wheels over and continues: "Your day and your garage have something important in common, son. They both need to be filled." My dad often talks in aphorisms, some from the Bible and some from his mind. "And it doesn't matter how big your garage is. You can build a ten-car garage, and one day you're going to come home with your eleventh car. With no place to put it." And then, as though sharing life's darkest secret with his youngest child, whom he never had a chance to raise, he adds, "That's just how it is."

It's the first helpful thing my dad's told me since my plane touched down: We're all just filling time with one another's problems.

I walk away again, and try to think only of Kate. How she's the only one in the world who calls me Hunt—my middle name— and the only one who understands that any family either of us ends up in—whether it's with Roger or with Jane—is going to be a little like *this*.

Roger walks in wearing a Hawaiian shirt and Birkenstocks, followed by the preacher in his black frock, dressed—just as I am—the same for weddings and funerals. They're followed by Roger's mom, Rhonda, and DD, her lover.

The preacher shakes Kate awake.

Corinne props Kate's head on a pillow and does her wedding makeup as only the president of Facade can: beautifully, yet with the speed and precision of a one-woman pit crew at the Indy 500, framing Kate's face like a Madonna with a burgundy shawl embroidered in gold. Finally, she gives her the bridal bouquet. Red roses, a spray of baby's breath, orange and yellow accents— romantic, nostalgic, dramatic in a way that suites Kate to a T. They really are sisters.

The nurse walks in to witness the ceremony, to make sure Kate isn't being coerced.

My dad stands up, letting out his equine whinny, a unique, disturbing tremolo resulting from his back injury. He trundles over to Kate and says, "Sweetheart?" Kate lifts up off the bed and hugs him and starts crying. Then my dad starts crying. "It's going to be all right," he tells her. "I love you so much."

Roger takes Kate's hand.

The preacher starts reading like an auctioneer: "Dearly beloved, we are gathered here to join this man and this woman in holy matrimony. . . ." Because he needs to finish before Kate falls back asleep.

When the preacher gets to the vows, Kate says, "I do."

My dad looks at Roger and shakes his hand.

My mom gives Roger a hug.

It's their finest hour as my parents, it seems to me, behaving with grace and warmth and dignity. I would have loved to have grown up in a family like this.

I uncork Corinne's fancy regifted champagne and fill the paper cups from the water dispenser.

Kate says, "I may be dying, but I want my fucking glass!" And then: "Shut that little brat up!" She doesn't realize that the infant down the hall who is crying incessantly is not a visitor, but a patient. Why spoil the party with the truth?

We all drink a toast to the bride and groom.

Then someone says, "How about a picture of the kids?"

I stand in the corner on one side of Kate's bed, and Corinne and Earl stand on the other, and we pose, facing a giant poster of the same pose taken twenty years ago, at Corinne's wedding; it's the only photograph ever taken of the four of us together as adults. There's a ten-year spread between me and my brother and sisters, and by the time I grew up, my mom was on to husband number four. The man in the family usually takes the pictures, but Norman didn't feel the need to record the shared history of his stepchildren, one of the many invisible costs of divorce. Corinne had it enlarged and then tacked it to Kate's wall to remind her where she came from.

I just stand there, my mother and father looking on, posing for the last picture that will ever be taken of us, looking at how we all used to look—Kate in her red dress, eyes scrunched, exploding in laughter, so full of life you can almost hear her; Corinne, regal and radiant in a peach silk dress and dazzling smile, looking every inch the girl who would move to Hollywood to take acting classes and become a star; Earl standing at one end in an impeccably tailored handmade suit, looking off at an angle, not one to pose, but smiling broadly into relaxed matinee-idol dimples that made girls ring our doorbell; and me, just home from college, before I wore glasses, the unlined and undefined face of a young man still becoming, overwhelmed by the powerful charisma and intensity and shared history standing next to me—but with a power of my own: Jane, of whom I could not have been more proud to call my new girlfriend. All of us are together in the same room, for the first time I can ever remember, and probably the last. Because of Kate. Who has brought us all together, and is showing us all, how hard it is, but how beautiful it can be, for each of us, in our different ways, to let go.

THIRTY

Ghostbuster

She's my girl
In her world
—song, year nineteen

A few weeks later, I'm back home in Copperfield, sitting in my office and staring out the window, when my mom calls.

"Kate died today, honey. At two-twenty-four."

After the wedding, the medical director of the hospice told me, "Go home, James. Live your life. So that Kate can live hers. And end it. Which she can't do with you living in her room, staring at her all the time. Dying in real life is not like it is on TV, James. Dying in real life is . . . *embarrassing.* It's like . . . going to the bathroom on the fifty-yard line . . . during the Super Bowl! And who's gonna do that?"

He's writing a book called *Negotiating with Your Angels.* It's about how, when your angels come to take you away, you ask for a little more time to work things out. But Kate kept on negotiating. She didn't want to 'go home.'

And I didn't want to go home.

But here I am, sitting in my office, staring out the window, wondering, Who am I going to tell that my sister just died?

I knew this was coming, so there should not be any surprise. But where there's life, there's hope, and as long as Kate was alive, part of me kept hoping for a miracle. The same part of me that hoped my psychotherapist would have sex with me in her office and help me work through my desire to have sex with other women. Stranger things have happened. You read stories all the time about mental-health professionals who are crazier than their patients. Just as you read stories about patients making miraculous recoveries from cancer. My mom was diagnosed with terminal cancer—and she proved the doctors wrong. Why not Kate?

And for that matter, why not my marriage? Couldn't we come back from the brink and prove wrong the thirteen couples counselors who had failed us and the dozens of friends who had stopped calling us and those on both sides of the family who had stopped visiting us? Death makes everything clear that way. You know this is it. This is who you are. Speak now, or forever hold your peace.

I walk downstairs to the kitchen and open the refrigerator and mention to Jane in a "We need more milk" kind of tone, "Kate died."

Jane, to her credit, tries to hug me. But accepting comfort from someone with whom you feel uncomfortable is a genuine challenge, even in a moment of genuine need. Added to this is the fact that Jane never accepted Kate for who she was: a nymphomaniac, alcoholic, thieving, junkie, pathological liar, hilarious genius. My patience for Kate's foibles was far greater than Jane's patience. I saw Kate's light amid her darkness. And I begrudged Jane her wise judgment.

"I loved Kate," Jane says. "I just didn't feel comfortable around her."

When Kate was married to her second husband, Jane and I flew out to Maui for the celebration. Kate had promised a splendid week of events: one night on the beach just for girls; another for out of towners; a rehearsal dinner; and of course the wedding. Half of this never materialized, which we learned on a day-to-day basis: The day of the girls night out came and then it went without the girls going out at night. Jane, understandably, was disappointed, and confused. "Why would she invite us and then not do it?" she asked. I said, "Because that's who she is." Still, I confronted Kate during a phone call. Kate said, "I am *not* a liar! I'm *exuberant*." At the rehearsal dinner, Kate arrived very late and lubricated. As we got into our separate cars, I said, "See you tomorrow." She said, "You still helping with the reception?" Kate, who ran a catering company, was catering it herself. I had offered to be a prep cook as a wedding present, expecting to prep at the beginning of the week. I said, "You said everything was done!" She said, "I lied. Nothing's done." She had a guest list of 250. The next morning at dawn, Jane and I arrived at Kate's house on the beach. In her prep kitchen were stacked coolers. In the coolers were frozen New Zealand lobster tails. Each one had to be scooped out—for starters. Two hours later, fingers frozen and bleeding, Jane collapsed on a cooler in anxiety and fatigue. "I can't do this," she said. "I didn't come to Maui to do this. It's too much." I agreed with her. I understood Kate's code; I *shared*

Jane's. That's one reason I married her. But Kate was my sister. And she had 250 people expecting to eat grilled lobster in mango sauce in a few hours. Mental health professionals might call this enabling: helping a person climb out of a self-destructive hole they dig themselves into, and in the process sustaining a nonsustainable way of living. In my family, this is a form of love. I stayed at my frozen lobster station, joined by employees and friends of Kate, whose collective efforts Kate orchestrated over the day like a conductor of a symphony orchestra, somehow coaxing us to perform at her frantic, lightning speed. A few minutes before her wedding on the beach in front of her house, she showered and changed into her gown, sat for makeup, and donned a flower tiara. Outside on the folding chairs, Jane and I sat together, exhausted, angry, and, at least in my case, in awe; Kate was a freak of nature. That's one reason why I saw her so few times over the years, and the same reason I loved and admired her. I wished that I could have shared my love of Kate with Jane. But Jane, perhaps prudently, saw that this way of life could not be sustained, and admired it from afar, which is perhaps one reason why Jane is still alive and mourning Kate.

We sit on the floor of the kitchen, the four of us, in a circle, with me facing Jane, Julian and Ben between us. We light a candle. We say a prayer, Jane and I connected to each other, through our children, for a moment.

Pretty soon, everything's back to normal. Ben is sitting on Jane's lap on the couch, breast-feeding—like any four-year-old boy who still breast-feeds. Julian is sitting next to them, his free hand clutching Jane's free nipple like a toggle switch to prove to Ben he still has nipple-access privileges—like any six-year-old boy who prefers holding a nipple to shooting a slingshot. Like it's any other day.

I walk downstairs to the basement, which is as far away as I can get from all this without actually running away from home.

When Jane comes down to do the laundry, I say, "I can't take it anymore. There are too many nursing first graders and frozen placentas and leprechauns in this house!" (One of the books on Jane's bedside table is entitled *My Summer with the Leprechauns: A Memoir.* She says she's reading it with a healthy suspicion.) "I'm sorry, but it's just weird. I don't even know you anymore!"

"I'm weird?" says Jane, continuing to load the washer—women are multitaskers, even in the heat of domestic battle. *"I'm* weird? Only one of us had a psychiatrist who was reincarnated!"

"That's because *I* helped *him* in his past life!"

"If you'd just let me be," she says, "we'd be fine." This is Jane's nod to Shakespeare, whom she knows I revere: Love alters not what love finds. Unfortunately for her, and for me, and therefore for us, Shakespeare in his infinite genius left the exceptions to love on the cutting room floor—among them, nursing first graders and freezing human organs.

"Do what you need to do," I say. "Do what you need to do. But this isn't any fun."

"Fun? *Fun*?!" The way she says 'fun'—only a German could be so appalled by the notion of pleasure as an essential ingredient of a painful relationship, it occurs to me. She's a purist, my wife; I'll grant her that. "What do you think this is, a game? Marriage is work!"

"I know it's work," I say. "I've been to thirteen marriage counselors! But I just saw my sister get married. On her death-bed. Laughing! She had a sense of humor. I have a sense of humor. *We* don't have a sense of humor, and it makes me want to die. I don't want to feel that anymore!"

"I'm sorry you feel that way," says Jane, turning on the wash-ing machine and gliding back upstairs in her enraging, "I prac-tice the turn the other cheek wisdom that Jesus preaches" way. Like she knows better. (Maybe she does know better!?) Like she's above it all. (Maybe she is above it all! Maybe I really *am* emotionally (and psychologically) (*and* spiritually) arrested?) I can't speak in a language Jane can understand, that much is cer-tain, and I have trouble understanding hers. And the gap be-tween us seems to keep widening. For good reason: The wooden floor around her organic cotton bed is ringed with stacks of spiritual development guides and self-help books and autobiog-raphies of mystics, some of whom I wouldn't be surprised to discover she may actually have been in past lives; not to men-tion, My Summer with the Leprechauns: A Memoir. The house is filled with journals and loose papers and little scraps with notes to herself, written in the same distinctive practical yet feminine script she used to write her name and number on the bottom of "The Devils You Know" on the night we met, to remember spiri-tual pearls she comes across when reading and talking for hours on end with girlfriends on the phone and at workshops and retreats. She's in a constant state of dialogue with herself and those around her about the meaning of Life, with a capital L. Versus me, a lowercase guy primarily asking the questions food? shelter? sex? Not in that order. Plus, Jane grew up in a house where to survive psychologically and emotionally she made a lifesaving choice early on to be unbreakable. Which to me often feels unbendable. Between the content she's absorbed in decades of emotional and spiritual training, and the nature of her character formed in the cauldron of a difficult childhood, I will *never* change Jane's unique, fascinating, infuriating mind. Why do I even try?

I hear Jane upstairs with the kids, running back and forth across the floorboards. It's a very comforting, homey sound.

Until I hear drums at the front door. Rainbow Feather is here, a visiting exorcist touring the country with her Peruvian stones, come to make our house safe from dark spirits.

A few nights ago, we'd been awakened by a bat, which (if you've never experienced a bat flying back and forth in the darkness across your bedroom) is essentially a blind mouse with wings, a flying mole, frantically trying escape the room into which it had flown. After Jane ejected me from under the covers of the family bed, where the four of us had sought shelter ("You're supposed to be the man!" she screamed at me as I squealed in fear along with the kids at the sound of the flapping wings overhead. "Do something!"), I taped a flashlight to a broom handle and suspended it out the open window to draw the bat outside. I didn't realize it was the open window and not the light that would draw the bat. Jane intuited that the bat was possibly not just a bat, but the reincarnated grandmother of the former owner of our new house. She had broken her neck descending the stairs one night, and evidently was not at peace—so she flew back to the scene of the crime. I on the other hand thought that the spirit might be Kate's, come to remind me of what we'd

talked about in the hospice—the potential point of disagree-
ment with Jane not being whether there's a ghost flying around
our house, but whose ghost it is. Jane and I really *are* well suited
to live with each other, at least in a psychiatric hospital. But I
kept my ghost theory to myself; I didn't want to get into another
argument.

Whoever the bat was, Rainbow Feather is here to clean up
the spiritual mess.

I was a little suspicious when Jane first told me about Rainbow Feather. Just as Jane is biased against nymphomaniac, alcoholic, thieving, junkie, pathological liar, hilarious geniuses, I have
a hard time accepting anyone who uses Rainbow as a proper
name, especially before Feather. We all have our prejudices.
Plus, I had never written a check with "Exorcist" in the memo
line before. But when Jane told me, "Pay to the order of Janet
Goldstein," Rainbow Feather's legal name, I let the drums roll.
Even exorcists need to make a living in the material world, I reasoned. We're all just doing the best we can.

I walk upstairs, and Rainbow Feather Goldstein asks me to
take the kids outside. "Play with them on the lawn, and keep
them away from the open windows," she says. "That's where the
spirits exit the house."

Jane, like a true mate, reads the bubble caption over my head
without my having to say anything. "Dark spirits attach to weak
spirits," she says.

I take the boys outside and kick around a soccer ball.

Julian asks, "Why are we playing soccer in the winter?"

I say, "Because I love you." Which is true. Leaving out "And
your mother believes that you and your brother will be cursed if

you don't stay ten feet from the poltergeist exit ramp. And I'm not sure whether she's crazy or gullible or highly intuitive. And since I'm a ball of fear and gullibility, as well as conflict-averse, and she may well have been right about the mercury tuna on our beach vacation, it's better to err on the side of Mommy's intuition."

Ben kicks a ball toward the house.

"Don't get near the window! I'll get it!" I scream, sounding like a superstitious maniac—which at this point, I have become.

I look at the windows hard, hoping to see the spirits. Would they really try to attach to the children? Would they really try to attach to me? Has it already happened?

I take the boys by the hand and lead them down the path to the farm at the bottom of the hill.

The air is clean. The sky is blue. The cows are spread out on the pasture below, grazing peacefully, the silo rising above the red barn.

I've done my job. I've helped bring two beautiful children into the world, and given them *this*. I feel the weight of their hands in mine, their warmth, their joy.

I feel my sister, out there.

I feel myself.

All of us are happy, it seems to me—even if one of us is technically dead. Maybe Jane is happy, too, back home, managing the exorcism. I can never be sure. She certainly likes her job— that much is clear. And maybe that's all you can ask out of life— to like your work. And I love being a father.

The problem is, I am also a husband.

THIRTY-ONE

Afterbirth and Death

You are like a starfish swimming through the waves
When somebody cuts you, you swim away
You are out there somewhere, trying to make it right
You are like a starfish, baby, you grow back and shine
—song, year twenty

I'm sitting in a circle on the ground under a stand of oak trees, with my family—Jane, Julian, Ben—saying a prayer for the placenta. After four years in the freezer—actually, three freezers; or maybe, between renovating our kitchen in New York and then renting two places up here before we bought our house, *five* freezers; not to mention the cooler we filled with dry ice to transport the placenta, like a medevac unit with an organ donation, which it was—it's finally underground, under a Canadian rosebush I bought at the Agway to mark the spot, in case we want to come back and pay our respects. (A buried placenta is like a pot of gold up here in Copperfield, where some people really do believe in leprechauns; if you ever want to find it again, you need to stash it under something that stands out amid the foliage.)

It took me three days to dig the grave. There's a layer of permafrost in upstate New York. And if you don't want to see your placenta dug up and carted off in the mouth of a fox or a coyote or a raccoon—or just by your dog or cat—you have to dig deep through the frozen layer, which is hell in the fall. Part of me wanted to wait until the spring thaw, but a bigger part of me couldn't go through another winter opening the freezer and seeing a human organ in a plastic tub. So when I drove up from New York this weekend, I grabbed the pick and shovel and started digging. Now I have the blisters to prove it.

In Jane's defense, she proposed we bury it months ago. But it was never convenient. I was always in the city, working. Or when I was up here, I wanted to play with the boys, instead of spending the day digging a grave, even a small one. Even though, as Jane pointed out, it would have taken a lot less time to dig it in the summer.

And when she'd suggest burying it without me, when I was down in the city, saying that the boys could dig the grave, I'd say no, citing an unwritten rule that unless you've run afoul of a Mexican drug cartel, a boy should not dig his own organ grave, or (if you're Julian) the grave for his brother's organ, or (in my sons' case) the grave for their mother's organ, if you're in the camp that considers that a placenta belongs to the mother, not the child. And anyway, I wanted to be there and dig the grave myself. We'd come a long way together, the placenta and I. I'd inflated the kiddie pool that allowed the placenta to come into the world with my own breath. I'd bought the plastic tub myself in the housewares section at Zabar's. And now I wanted to finish what I started on the day Ben was born, when I put the placenta in the freezer.

Given my schedule, this meant delaying the burial again and

again. Which allowed the placenta, like that extra pound or two (or three-quart container), to become easier and easier to live with, less and less embarrassing, less "not me." Then I realized *it was me*; I'd grown attached to the thing. I didn't want to bury it. It made me feel *special*. Who else has a four-year-old, three-quart human organ in their freezer? And it was part of our life together in the city, the last vestige of our truly shared history, Jane's and mine, before I started coming up here only on weekends, leaving Jane alone with the kids during the week, when she did things alone and I did things alone and, as a result, Jane became less and less recognizable to me, both as the woman I'd spent half my life with and as the woman with whom I was willing to spend the rest of it.

When Jane was in seminary, there was a visiting student from Africa staying at the end of her hall. "In my village," he joked, "this is where we put the person who the tiger eats, so the rest of us are warned." It was an allusion to the fact that if someone broke into the building, they'd kill him first, so the rest of us could make a getaway. He loved New York, he said, crime and all. But it was changing him so much that he was flying his wife over from Africa to be with him for the second semester. "We need to go through this experience together," he said. "If you go through something like this alone, you will never understand that part of each other. And you will grow apart."

Burying the placenta meant recognizing that our shared life, whatever we'd gone through together, was past, and that it was time to look at the present, so we could figure out the future.

On a bright, hopeful morning, three days after I began digging the hole deep enough to keep a fox from digging it up, Jane took the container out of the freezer and set it on the kitchen counter to thaw.

A few hours later, we all trundled down the hill to the oak trees, Jane carrying the tub. We chose the burial site originally for the tree fort when we first moved up here. But eventually it became the abandoned tree fort, only you can't tell whether it's in the process of being built or of decaying. I'm not especially handy. And sinking support posts in the permafrost is even harder than digging a grave. So I made it only as far as screwing a few two-by-fours into the tree trunks and dangling a plumb line down from one beam into the brush. If I pick the project back up, it will be on hallowed ground.

Jane peeled back the lid to the tub and plopped the semi-thawed contents into the grave.

The boys looked away. "Euew!" said Ben at the squishy, wet sound of the thing that once had been attached to him, and literally gave him life.

"Disgusting," said Julian, older and thus more verbal.

I said nothing. They'd said it all.

Jane said nothing, but I thought I could see a slight wincing on her face. This squishy, wet brown thing came out of her, after all.

I shoveled in some dirt right away. Then I pulled out the rose-bush to transplant.

The boys grabbed their kid-size shovels and helped me fill the grave.

Then the four of us sat down in a circle, held hands, and said a prayer for Ben, led by Jane—"May he have a long, beautiful life"—just as we'd said a prayer when Kate died, a few months before. I could never do this on my own, it occurs to me. Never. Not with any conviction anyway. I outsource my spiritual life to Jane. Just as she outsources grave digging to me, at least when there's permafrost.

And now here we are, the four of us, looking at the Canadian rosebush, just as Jane and I were looking at one when our cat Omar died, many years ago. That's when I first used a Canadian rosebush to mark a grave—and, for that matter, first used a cooler to transport a frozen mammal, or part thereof. Omar died at the vet's in Brooklyn, and we picked her up from his deep freeze, put her on dry ice, drove her to Jane's dad's on the Cape, and thawed her for a few days at the foot of our bed in a cat wake— frozen cats look a lot like sleeping cats, in case you haven't seen one. Then we buried her under a Canadian rosebush, like this one, with only a piece of rustic burlap that we'd ripped from a tacky pine-scented pet pillow to line Omar's communion with the earth. We'd searched for days as Omar thawed at the foot of our bed for the perfect final resting vessel. The plastic cooler was too durable: Like most things made of polypropylene it had a half-life of probably 2,000 years. Omar's body wouldn't break down for centuries at best, and in fact given how good that cooler was she might remain frozen for millennia, a ghoulish cat mummy to some unsuspecting kid digging around his back-yard in the distant future. The LL Bean shoebox was too dis-connected: Omar didn't wear shoes. The cushion from the cat store filled with fake pine-scented foam—Omar never would have liked that scent in life. Nothing measured up to her pri-mal dignity. So we just kept searching for the perfect way to say good-bye. It was hard to let her go. I loved that cat. I love our cats.

"Where's Hamster?" I say, the boys' name for one of their gerbils, *gerbil* being a word they hate, hence Hamster and Mouse, their other gerbil. The last time I saw Hamster was a few minutes ago, on the bed in the bedroom (there's no such thing as a master bedroom when everyone sleeps in the same bed), with Jane and Ben, who was playing with Hamster before we headed down to the grave site.

Jane says, "I don't know."

I say, "You don't *know*?"

Ben says to Jane, "You said you'd put him away!"

I say, "Where are the cats?" Muff and Puff, who (unlike Omar) are both buff—as various squirrel heads, dove beaks, and entrails that litter the landscape attest; as will the missing ear on the next-door neighbor's tom-cat, Irving, the former alpha, who belongs to the organic-cheese maker Everett and his wife. They may be able to eat human organs, but our cats can kick their cat's ass. Apart from the fact that they drink from a water bowl, Muff and Puff are essentially fierce, wild animals. The kind of animals who eat gerbils—and hamsters and mice—in one squirming bite.

We all run from the grave, cutting short the funeral for Ben's placenta, Ben in the lead, sprinting up the hill and into the house.

I have a sick feeling as I bring up the rear, and not just because my four-year-old and six-year-old can both outrun me.

From inside the house, Ben screams.

A few seconds later, he emerges at the door to the porch, hand outstretched. "You killed Hamster!" he screams at Jane. Behind him, Julian stands, tears streaming down his face; although older, he's still blessedly capable of sorrow, not just anger. He is my teacher.

I walk up the hill and collapse on the lawn, winded, livid. The boys sit on my lap, one on each leg, sobbing, Ben holding the stiff little fur pack in his palm. "You killed Hamster!"

Jane stands on the edge of the lawn, unable—unwelcome—to approach the boys.

I try to shift the conversation to cause of death; CSI Rodent. When faced with mortality, problem solving has a palliative effect. It gets your mind off the real problem: one day *you'll* be in someone's hand. By emotional alchemy, I want to turn unfathomable grief into a riddle. "There are no bite marks," I say. "Where did you find him?"

"Between the bed and the wall," says Ben.

It wasn't the cat! And technically it wasn't Jane. "He must have fallen in and had a heart . . ." I stop short of issuing the full coroner's report. "Poor little guy."

"He had a horrible life inside that cage," says Jane, who had discouraged the boys from getting gerbils to begin with. The only way to stop the suffering of future generations of rodents in their smelly little prison cells, she reasoned, was to make sure they are never born to begin with, and that meant letting all domestic rodents die in pet stores.

"You didn't have to kill him!" says Julian.

Jane is visibly stricken. "It's Ben's pet," she says, "not mine."

"It's a *rodent*," I say finally. "In a house with *cats*." Hoping Jane will do the math. But just in case . . . "You can't leave a four-year-old in charge." Even though, when she was four years old, she *may* have been in charge. Girls grow up faster, especially in Germany.

"What could I have done?" asks Jane earnestly.

"Put Hamster in the cage before you came downstairs to bury the placenta." Which is basically what I told Jane upstairs, when I saw Ben playing with Hamster on the family bed before the family funeral.

"I guess you're right," says Jane, and she walks back into the house.

It's a stunning end to a fight that could have gone on for hours, for days, for twenty years. That she didn't know this to begin with, that she's now admitted she didn't know it, and, most of all, that she says I'm *right*! leaves me literally speechless—and deeply sad. Not that Hamster died. Which is sad, but mainly for the boys—and for Hamster. I'm sad that Jane didn't tell me this twenty years ago. Or last year. Or yesterday. That she didn't take the hit in moments where it clearly was her fault. Didn't say, simply, "I'm sorry" and move on, and instead invariably found a way to pin the blame on me, or, at the absolute most, to say, "It's not about blame, James!" Which of course it *is* about, if you're married to me, and in any case is very easy to say when it's your fault and you are trying to avoid taking the blame. It's a way to sound vaguely principled, when really you're scared and simply trying to deflect attention. It's a maddening personality trait— especially when both of you possess it. For I, too, am a master of pinning the blame on Jane for things that really are my fault. And who wants to look in the mirror when something so enraging is going to look back? So I've obfuscated and counterblamed and principle-feigned ("It's not about blame, Jane!") in return,

which has led to endless looping arguments, simply because neither of us can ever be the first to say "I'm sorry."

I seriously think that in the last twenty years, Jane has told me
"You're right" fewer times than she's said, "Let's have mind-
blowing sex." And she's never said, "Let's have mind-blowing
sex." Sex is not how we blow each other's minds.

We blow each other's minds through mind-blowing conflict.
We can argue literally about anything: Should a rug really be
called a "carpet"? Is it better to turn left or right on a bike ride
through Central Park? Are the paintings in the Metropolitan
Museum fakes, forged by the Met after they bought the real
things, which they keep locked in a vault, away from thieves and
vandals, and people, (like me), standing inches from supposedly
real forty-million-dollar paintings with a definitely real Swiss
Army Knife in my pocket, or am I just being paranoid and de-
lusional? (Maybe Jane *was* right about this one.)

For Jane to say I'm right after twenty years of *this* takes real
guts. Which makes me love her and admire her, and fall silent.

At the bottom of the hill, under the oak tree, looking down at
the Canadian rosebush atop the placenta, finally interred under
a fresh burial mound, shovels and spades scattered around the
grave site, the gerbil soon to follow, the boys up where the hill
plateaus in the yard, kicking a ball, Jane in the kitchen, all is
well. We have nothing more to fight about, really. The past is
buried. Unless the coyotes dig it up. So I just stand there, listening to the birds—sparrows, crows, a woodpecker . . . local, seasonal, organic music . . . wrapped in the toxic mainstream noise
of distant highway hum.

Or maybe . . . it's tinnitus. I should have stuck to writing love poems, or worn earplugs when I started playing electric guitar in my high school rock band. You never believe it will happen to you. Then it happens to you, you *make* it happen, ears cursed for the rest of your life with satanic reverb. Sometimes, I'm so upset by the choices I've made I can't decide whether I'm suicidal or homicidal—whether I should end it all, or kill you. What was I *thinking*?!

But today, this endless looping *ring* feels like a strange gift: a built-in alarm *I* installed that I can never turn off, consequences of choices I made long ago echoing across time, reminding me to always pay attention: Are those birds singing? Or are they signaling other birds: Fly away before the cats eat you, too? It's easy to mistake pain for pleasure, when you're me. But I'm getting better at telling the difference between the two. And with one gerbil dead, the other in the rodent witness protection program, and two hungry cats, whereabouts unknown, now would be a good time to fly.

ACKNOWLEDGMENTS

This story started out on the stage. Along the path to the page, I benefitted from the ideas and support of many people, most of whom I will forget to recognize. To you I am about to offend (and you know who you are, as well as I don't), please know in advance that I am sorry. My mind is often afraid of noting the many people who have helped me in ways large and small. Meaning, forgetting to mention you here is just me being me: as grateful as I am humbled by my need, terrified that I don't have forever to acknowledge it and therefore avoiding note-taking along the way, thinking I'll always have tomorrow to remember. Self-absorption is a childlike state, and children think they will live forever. Growing up, as this book will attest, is hard to do.

First and foremost, thanks to The Moth in New York City for giving me a stage on which to tell my stories, a warm and interesting audience to tell them to, a community of supportive fellow storytellers who challenged me to be my best, and ultimately a place to change my life. Led by Joey Xander and then by Lea Thau and Catherine Burns, who possesses a work ethic so formidable that it would be scary were it not rivaled by her deep Southern warmth and compassion, along with the clothes horse/ workhorse extraordinaire Sarah Austin Jenness, The Moth is for me the single brightest spot in New York City. It's where I went when my sister died to feel the comfort of community. It's where I first told the story of her death. It's a home, in the best way.

Thanks to the hilarious, brilliantly irreverent Jenifer Hixson, amazing producer of The Moth Slams, for giving me excellent, supportive critique over many years, for suggesting that I develop my stories in print (partly to stop bugging her for stage time), and for being the only person I have ever met who in one word and gesture can become a character, someone else entirely, then change back into herself, without making anyone feel put upon, because it *always* serves the story. Hers is a humbling gift, used with deep humility, which never fails to inspires me.

Thank you Victoria C. Rowan, whose outstanding skills as a veteran writing workshop leader, inspiring private writing coach, and superb manuscript editor profoundly changed the trajectory of my work and my life. Her gimlet critique of my early show script and book chapters was almost as irritating as the life I was living that inspired my stories. Her thoughtful, thorough, and informed comments engaged me, enraged me, and ultimately inspired me to rethink my writing, and substantially improve it. May all storytellers be lucky enough to have Victoria guide their project to a better place. Thanks also for unholstering the second-to-none Rolodex, calling upon a veritable national database of friends and associates to people my show as it traveled across the country.

Thank you to the myriad members of Victoria Rowan's writing workshops over the years. Your comments inspired me to write better—and your book deals agitated me to work harder.

Thanks to Ted Lorenz for suggesting we go downtown one night in my twenties to see a man named Spalding Gray performing an autobiographical monologue, and then years later, as I complained about being me, for saying, "Write about what makes you angry."

Thanks to John Werber, MD, for helping me develop my voice, through unflappable patience, methodical scientific curiosity, and flat-out twisted voyeurism. Hundreds of hours of extemporaneous stories took shape in response to John's oft-repeated interlocution, "You're *kidding*?" Followed by, "And *then* what happened?"

Thank you Jim Florack and Tracy Kimmel, for turning their attentions from tremendously demanding professional lives to nurture my dream, invest in my show, and help bring my story to the stage in New York City.

Thank you Tom Weiser for signing on as my best man, knowing (as a mythology major) that a best man's primordial job is to marry my wife in case I go missing. Thanks also for being a gifted storyteller with enough practical organizational ability to bring together a group of storytellers and form Hearsay, giving me another community within which to grow.

Thanks to everyone in Hearsay, whose motto "Free to Suck" gave me permission to fail, one of the greatest gifts a storyteller can possess: Alternate Ithaca Tom Weiser, whose story of what might have been never fails to resonate deep within my ambivalent mind and heart; Catherine "Don't Hate Me for Having Been a Hot Stripper" Burns, who can tell a story as well as she can help others tell theirs; Jenifer "Am I Wrong to worry about a man who still lives with his mother?" Hixson, whose alchemical capacity to transform misadventures into comic narrative gold are legend among those privileged to have been there; Mary Domowicz, who, what with her mnemonic devices for remembering the capitals of all fifty states may be weirder than I am, but who is clearly orders of magnitude hotter in a miniskirt, so it doesn't matter; Micheala Murphy, who tells stories like my sister K: with tremendous heart, a brilliant command of the language, and a deep love of her characters, and who possesses the genuine curiosity of a child and the moxie of a woman who can get herself into (and out of) situations rich enough to produce amazing tales; and of course to Jeffrey Rudell, whose ramrod posture and exemplary fitness inspires physical envy, and whose carefully crafted stories inspire deep respect for his singular attention to the telling detail and a truly extraordinary capacity to polish work to a glistening finish—I am almost glad I lost to him in those storytelling competitions at The Moth many nights ago.

Thanks to Andy Christie for major league help during the production of the very first workshop performance of my show at the old Dixon Place, and for listening to so many iterations of my stories that he came to understand what it felt like to be me, not easy for anyone.

Thanks to Sherry Weaver and her Speakeasy Stories, a stage where Sherry told us anything goes . . . and anything went, beginning with the most wonderfully bizarre performer introductions *ever*.

Thanks to Jean-Michelle Gregory for her early notes and to Mike Daisey for the gift of his troubled rubbery face after the first workshop performance, as he struggled for a way to tell me, "Oh my god . . ." in a supportive way that led me to question some of my artistic assumptions.

Thank you Gregory Mosher, for telling me, "You get to tell your story because other people are afraid to tell theirs. They will explore their lives through yours. If you don't have the courage to tell the truth, you can't do this work." It was a hard truth, especially as Gregory, a stage director, not a writer, had no intention of following it! But he knew of what he spoke and he was absolutely right.

Thank you Lisa Ford for whispering more or less the same thing in my ear on stage after an otherwise rousing curtain call at Ars Nova, reminding me that in this kind of art, truth trumps applause.

Thank you Hal Brooks for telling me in our first rehearsal, "My job is not to laugh. My job is to pay attention, take notes, and make you stronger." Mission accomplished.

Thanks Sarah Jones for not only *not* complaining that I filched her e-mail and solicited her out of the blue, but for coming to opening night and bringing friends, extending herself to a total stranger. Such acts of generosity are rare, and I am humbly grateful for her kindness when it really mattered.

Thanks Andy Borowitz for coming to a workshop, then meeting me for lunch at Jackson Hole and telling me, "You have to decide, do you want it to be a bunch of funny stories? Or do you want it to add up to something more?" That was the most clarifying burger and fries *ever*.

Thanks to Jonathan Ames for sharing his post-show confusion over a missing detail. It was a telling lapse on my part that led to me looking at my whole monologue with an eye toward clarifying many more such questions before it was too late.

Thanks Ars Nova for giving me a stage on which to workshop my material before going to the Fringe in Edinburgh.

Thanks Louise Chantal and the Assembly Rooms in Edinburgh for one of the great experiences of my life, providing a crucible in which the elements of my story finally coalesced, and to the journalists Steve Cramer and Adrian Turpin for making the effort to see what I was really trying to accomplish.

Thanks to the anonymous taxi driver in Edinburgh who asked me how my show was going, and when I told him, "Not well," told me that when it came to viewing autobiographical monologues people in Edinburgh did not possess ironic detachment, inspiring me to write a thirty-second introduction that changed everything.

Thank you Elysabeth Kleinhans and Peter Tear at 59 E 59 Theater, for sitting in the front row in Edinburgh and approaching me after the show when I stepped out of the broom closet, which doubled as the backstage, and inviting me to perform at their fabulous theater New York City.

Thank you Ira Glass, Nancy Updike, Seth Lind, and the rest of the gang at *This American Life*, for sharing a story from my show with their unique, amazing audience.

Thanks to Maggie da Silva, who published early autobiographical stories in her magazine *Gooch!* giving me the confidence that someone might want to read more.

Thanks to Albert Stern, for listening to me perform for sixty minutes alone in his conference room on the thirty-fifth floor, burning his lunch hour and risking his credibility with his employer, then giving me thoughtful post-performance critique *in writing*.

Thanks Robin Hirsch at Cornelia Street Café for spreading the word at a critical moment.

Thanks Melissa Bank, Dan Kennedy, and Joyce Maynard for enthusiastic words of support.

Thank you Leslie Strongwater at Dixon Place for listening to my first performance while working in the backroom and then e-mailing me the loveliest, most inspiring fan note ever—not least because she called me mister.

Thank you Anna Becker, for approaching me at The Moth after I first performed my story about the death of my sister, for believing me when I said that yes I did have a whole show, not just a story, for producing an early workshop of the show that I wrote to make good on my claim to have already written a show, and then for producing the show Off-Broadway, always believing in me and communicating confidence in ways quiet and loud, leaving everyone in the room the dignity of their own opinion while moving the process forward.

Thank you Dani Klein Modisett for inviting me to the stage of her hilarious show *Afterbirth*, where I met my patient agent, Elisabeth Weed, and my wonderful editor at St. Martin's.

Thank you Elizabeth Beier for being first a fan, then a supportive friend, and finally, when I actually began to write my book, a brilliant editor capable of synthesizing scores of observations into a single, piquant comment that unlocked for what I was trying to say. As no good deed goes unpunished when publishing a tale such as mine, thank you also for besting Job in the patience department. This project took longer to bring to fruition than the construction of most New York skyscrapers, a fact perhaps not lost on her every time she looked out her office window and wondered whether and when I would be submitting my next chapter.

Thank you Michelle Richter, for keeping me (and Elizabeth!) on track, to the degree I can stay on a track.

Thank you to my sister for flying to New York for opening night and for greeting my tale with total enthusiasm and acceptance, and to my brother for graciously enduring a level of exposure that I know was never on his bucket list. In another life, he was a black cat who walked in the shadows along walls; he does not seek this kind of sunlight. I owe him sunglasses, and then some.

Thanks to my awesome nieces and nephew for gleefully spreading the news on social media about the story of the foibles of their elders.

Thank you to my children for continually reminding me what is important in life, including that my book was long overdue, and for suggesting which pseudonyms might best fit their personalities, which—this being a long-overdue book—changed along the way.

Thanks to my mom for believing in my show and not taking too much umbrage at the perhaps less-than-flattering moments, and instead saying with quiet confidence, "I know who I am."

Thanks to my dad for being the best raconteur I have ever heard, and showing me by example how one man standing in a living room using words alone can make an emotional impact as deep and powerful as any other form of art.

Thanks to my sister K, not only for whistling past the graveyard, but for performing in it, then coming to me one night and literally pulling me out of bed to awaken me to my responsibilities as a storyteller.

Thank you, Amy Rapp for being a patient and wise friend and a loyal colleague who (this being the business of storytelling) makes you suspend disbelief and think you are the only item on her To Do list, bringing a level of dedication and commitment not in any job description of a movie producer's responsibilities. Not content with developing my monologue into a TV show, Amy miraculously booked my national tour, and then produced it in local markets as it traveled the country, all while running a film and television production company in New York City catering to other writers who thought they were the only items on her To Do list and persuading her boss she hadn't lost her mind.

Thanks to Meredith Vieira for having so many more talents than I can ever hope to possess, including the wisdom to follow Amy Rapp's belief in me and the show!

Thanks to Little Johnny Koerber, Executive Producer of *Life in a Marital Institution*, for giving generously of his time, resources, energy, and heart: sharing his love of the Beatles, reminding me that the greatest popular art begins with great entertainment; venturing out in the snow to a tiny club in outer Brooklyn to see me perform seven minutes of material; treating me to an eye-opening education in solo shows, including thoughtful après theater critique; sending me to cut my theatrical teeth at the Edinburgh Fringe; bringing me back to live my dream Off Broadway; reassuring me in the back of the taxi awaiting my first reviews, that I had reached my goal; giving me an artistic mantra, which remains the sharpest, most helpful bit of feedback

I have yet received in years of creative development: "Bite off less and go deeper"; making myriad large and small contributions that together represent the single greatest act of generosity I have ever experienced and for which I will be forever grateful.

And finally, thank you to the woman I'll call Jane for driving me out of my mind, and into the uncharted and dangerous, exhilarating and beautiful and terrifying territory of the heart and soul. She showed me places I didn't know existed, that in some cases I would prefer to have left undiscovered, but that I would never have seen without her—and which, having experienced them, inspired me to tell a tale to try to understand her challenging nature (and mine, too) while, hopefully, conjuring her unique, childlike, and powerful spirit.